Better Homes and Gardens®

celebrate the SEASON

2002

Better Homes and Gardens® Books
Des Moines, Iowa

Better Homes and Gardens®
Celebrate the Season 2002

Editor in Chief: Beverly Rivers
Art Director: Trish Podlasek
Executive Editor Family Food Collection: Joy Taylor
Food Editor: David Feder, RD
Contributing Editor: Vicki Ingham
Contributing Food Writer: Wini Moranville
Contributing Decorating/Crafts Writer: Jilann Severson
Contributing Art Director/Graphic Designer: Marisa Dirks
Copy Editor: Peg Smith
Indexers: Janet Figg, Peg Smith
Assistant to the Editor in Chief: Lori Eggers

Vice President, Publishing Director: William R. Reed

Group Publisher: Maureen Ruth
Consumer Product Marketing Director: Ben Jones
Senior Consumer Product Marketing Manager: Steven Swanson
Consumer Product Marketing Manager: Karrie Nelson
Business Manager: Jie Lin
Production Manager: Douglas M. Johnston
Book Production Managers: Pam Kvitne, Marjorie J. Schenkelberg
Assistant to the Publisher: Cheryl Eckert

Chairman and Chief Executive Officer: William T. Kerr
Chairman of the Executive Committee: E. T. Meredith III

Meredith Publishing Group

Publishing Group President: Stephen M. Lacy
Magazine Group President: Jerry Kaplan
Corporate Solutions: Michael Brownstein
Creative Services: Ellen de Lathouder
Manufacturing: Bruce Heston
Consumer Marketing: Karla Jeffries
Finance and Administration: Max Runciman

For book editorial questions, write: *Better Homes and Gardens® Celebrate the Seasons,*
1716 Locust St., Des Moines, IA 50309-3023.

Cover photograph: Peter Krumhardt

Our seal assures you that every recipe in *Celebrate the Season* has been tested
in the Better Homes and Gardens® Test Kitchen. This means that each recipe is
practical and reliable and meets our high standards of taste appeal. We guarantee
your satisfaction with this book for as long as you own it.

gathering

family and friends to celebrate the holidays begins by reveling in the memories of seasons past. Many times throughout the year are spent recalling hours of fun creating and giving gifts, decorating for parties, baking and cooking delicious foods for special occasions, and enjoying visits with people whose company we cherish. Preparation for these welcome events is truly an important activity that paves the way for pleasant memories. The following pages are filled with decorating, gift-making, and food ideas and are bound to inspire your creativity. Throughout the book, **In a Twinkling** project ideas help to make the most of valuable time and resources during the holidays. To excite your taste buds, our food editors selected their favorite dessert recipes, see *pages 106–111*. For cookies, always important to holidays, see the assortment of cultural delights—from Florentines to Benne Cakes—on *pages 100–105*. Whatever your heritage, we invite you to celebrate, using ideas from around the world.

Beverly Rivers

— Beverly Rivers, Editor

For a fast and easy table decoration, gather clear glass containers from your cupboards and fill them with ornaments in colors that coordinate with your room's decor. Cluster them, making sure you select a variety of sizes and shapes. Tie sheer ribbon bows through the remaining ornaments and place one at each setting as a gift for the guest.

table *of* contents

setting the stage

gathering together

5

giving from the heart

kids' stuff

...and to all a good night

In a Twinkling

Easy-to-use ideas for the holidays

SETTING

Make the holidays more fun this year by creating beautiful decorations with some of the things you already have. Tuck greens and berries in and around your accessories—right where they sit. Embellish hanging light fixtures and table lamps. Add ribbons and ornaments to trees of all sizes—living, cut, and assembled from nature. Embellish candles with such items as buttons, wire, and leaves. Make and hang brown kraft paper cones filled with evergreen and berries. Start thinking now how to incorporate your favorite objects into centerpieces and mantel displays. Your personal style will shine through when you allow seasonal trims to work naturally with your year-round decorating. Enjoy your creativity.

the STAGE

Whether done in a larger-than-life display or a subtle touch here and there, winter greens instantly add festive appeal. Look for fresh mixed greens, then blend in a few unexpected items to take the displays from plain tree-lot wreaths and garlands to an arrangement worthy of a room's focal point.

green greeting

Even though a ring of greens is the traditional holiday greeting, there's no need to settle for a generic fir wreath with a simple red velvet bow. Create a wreath that matches your door as well as your holiday theme by adding items from a crafts store. Start with a basic wreath that's large enough to make an impressive impact from the street. Wedge snippets of other greens into the wreath, then top them with ribbons, ornaments, or other items. Wire or glue the decorations to the wreath for a focal point, then scatter a few more around the wreath.

legendary *greens*

Evergreens, holly, mistletoe, and other greenery are a mainstay of the holidays, adding a fresh touch to every room.

miniature trees

❧ Plant your own tiny forest of trees for a table or mantel display. Pick a selection of rustic clay pots for the bases, then match plastic foam cones to fit the bottoms of the pots.

Choose small fresh lemon, ivy, or salal leaves or their silk counterparts. Clip off the stems. If desired, mist or cover the leaves with gold spray paint. Starting at the bottom edge of the cone and working up, pin or hot-glue concentric rows of leaves around the cones, covering the base of each leaf with the tip of the leaf above it. Make a small cluster of leaves at the top for a crown, then add miniature ornaments and toppers. Place the pot on its rim and glue the cone to the bottom of the pot.

mistletoe light

❧ Gussy up a chandelier with mistletoe and sweetness. Wire small clusters of mistletoe to the candle cups, then cover the wires with bows. Hang candy canes from the arms (leave the paper on for protection and a bit of sparkle) and dangle glass candies from fine cords to catch and reflect the light.

sugarplum swag

Beads, balls, baubles, and bows bring magical colors all around an elegant mantel. The secret to arranging this display is a well-hidden box that holds the greens in place. For greatest impact, aim to create an arrangement with a center height equivalent to half the length of the mantel. Taper the height toward the ends of the mantel, then let the garland fall all the way to the floor along the sides.

here's how...

Make a base. Build or buy several small or one large box to fit your mantel. Cover the bottom with felt to prevent scratches. Line the bottom with floral foam and weight the back with bricks to keep it from tipping.

Finish the front. Add lacy greens such as juniper, cedar, and pine, letting them cascade over the box front. Interweave the greens, pins, and garland so all parts are secure. Trim the garland to brush the floor.

Fill it in. Insert tall fir branches into the foam, fanning them so the tallest ones are at the center. Lay a mixed-green garland over the box. Make giant U-shape pins from heavy floral wire to anchor the garland in place.

Add the trims. For bow clusters, bend floral wire into a U shape. Slide three balls to the end. Shape ribbon into a bow, slide it over the ball tops, and twist the wire to secure it. Wire the bow clusters and garlands in place.

floral kissing ball

❧ Mistletoe may be the mainstay for kissing balls; floral orbs, however, hold just as much magic and even more romance. Make orbs any size you want, using a plastic foam ball for the base. Then, as long as you're breaking with tradition, hang the kissing balls in more than just the front entrance. Hang them from doorknobs, furniture pulls, towel bars, and chandeliers.

To make the kissing balls, cover a plastic foam ball with moss using either crafts glue or U-shape floral pins to hold it in place. Snip flowers so short stems remain and pin them in place to cover the ball. Use sprigs of ivy and other cascading flowers to give the ball a less controlled shape. Pin a length of ribbon to the top of the ball, then add greens and roses around the base of the ribbon. If necessary, use small dots of hot glue to hold everything in place.

key tag garland

❧ Plain white metal-edge key tags from the office supply store become a charming little garland when a bit of paint and fabric-store trim are applied. They're the perfect size for an in-between tree that is too small for purchased garlands and too big for miniatures.

Dip the tags in water, then brush both sides with watercolor paint. Hang them to dry over a stack of newspapers. We used bright colors to contrast with the red-flocked tree, but any color scheme will work. After the paint dries, remove the hanging strings and slide the key tags onto ribbon or beaded trim, spacing them evenly.

12

initial wreath

ﻌ Put your mark on the front door with a wreath in the shape of your family initial. It's a great solution to personalize your home.

Cut large sheets of plastic foam in the shape of your initial. (Use computer fonts as a guide for the shape or draw your own.) If necessary, join several sheets of plastic foam by hot-gluing them together and using U-shape floral pins to further secure the seams. If desired, spray-paint the initial green with paint that is labeled as safe for use on plastic foam.

Cut small pieces of various greens. Using U-shape floral pins, completely cover the initial shape with greenery. To conceal the pins, attach one sprig under the ends of the next sprig. In areas that have mild climates, hot glue also can be used to secure the sprigs. Keep in mind that cold may cause the glue to become brittle and heat may soften the glue.

13

sugar-frosted topiary

A tabletop topiary takes on colonial style when packed with sweet treats. Highlight a fresh or silk ivy topiary with spray snow that is used to flock trees and greens. (The spray can be washed off later.) To sugar kumquats, clementines, pears, grapes, and other fruits for the topiary, dip them in beaten egg white diluted with a little water. Roll the fruit in superfine sugar to coat, and let the sugar coating dry on a wire rack. Skewer the fruit with heavy-gauge floral wire, clustering small fruits, and nestle them in the topiary. Arrange sugared fruits along the base of the arrangement.

arched swag

This unusual wreath is a winner, and so easy to do. Using heavy-duty wire cutters, remove one segment of a 24-inch diameter open-wire box wreath. Wrap a six-foot-long garland around the wreath form so it has double thickness. Hold the garland in place with floral wire. Attach a bow made from two yards of ribbon to the top. Add a glass ornament under the bow. Hot-glue white silk freesia, white roses, and pinecones around the bow to create an elegant focal point.

a christmas greenery primer

For generations, we've hung mistletoe in the entryway, swagged the stairway with greens, decorated trees, and tucked sprigs of holly around our homes. Bringing verdant greenery into the house has become a tradition shared by many cultures.

Although legends vary by country and culture, below are a few accepted histories regarding evergreens.

Wherever you use greenery, choose it fresh from reputable stores, florists, or tree lots. To check for freshness, bend the branches to check for discoloration and dryness. Greenery that is not fresh has loose or prickly needles or leaves, and branches or trunks may be painted or dyed. When you get greenery home, cut or saw off cut ends and water them well.

laurel

Ancient Romans believed laurels and other trees housed the gods of growth and rejuvenation. By providing safe shelter for the deity during cold winter months, householders believed they could harness life-promoting powers.

holly and ivy

Believed by Romans and early Christians to have protective powers, holly and ivy were symbols of love. Because both were used as charms throughout the house, we "deck the halls with boughs of holly."

green boughs

Year-round verdant evergreens hinted of supernatural powers for Greeks and Romans, who brought it indoors as a sign of vitality. The Victorians, however, made the use popular.

hawthorn

The story says that England's St. Joseph of Arimathea planted his staff, and from it hawthorn blossomed on Christmas Eve. One American variety produces red fruit all winter long.

mistletoe

When her son Balder was killed by an arrow of mistletoe, Frigga's tears turned to white mistletoe berries. This Norse goddess of love swore that mistletoe would from then on be a sign of love.

flowering branches

On December 13, St. Lucia's Day in Sweden, girls plant a cherry branch in wet sand. If the branch blooms before Christmas, they believe that all their holiday wishes will be fulfilled.

evergreen trees

The first record of decorated trees comes from the Alsace region of France. In 1605, a writer described how cut trees were dressed in apples, gold foil, paper roses, wafers, and sweets.

15

▶ Glass Charms. Guests will identify which drink is theirs by the colorful beads. Wrap a 4-inch eye pin around a $7/8$-inch dowel, the end of the pin overlapping the loop by $1/4$ inch. Clip off the excess and bend the end into a hook that will slip through the eye. String beads onto head pins and slide them onto the ring.

In a Twinkling
decorations

◀ Spell it Out. Express your sentiments in cookie-cutter fashion. Line a shelf, ledge, or bookcase with cookie cutters that spell seasonal messages. Look for inexpensive cookie cutters at discount kitchen stores. For interest, stagger, overlap, and slightly tip the letters. Keep the letters in place with poster adhesive or removable poster tape under each letter.

▼ Marble Platter. Turn a plain glass plate into a bauble-lined dessert or candle plate. Glue flat marbles, purchased from a floral department, to a smooth-rimmed plate using glass bonding glue. Lightly tape the marbles to keep them in place while the glue dries.

▲ To the Letter. Spell out wishes for the season with distinctively framed letters. Print large letters on a computer, then trace and cut them from corrugated art paper. Glue the letters to construction paper and frame them, omitting the glass. For interest, vary the size of both the letters and the frames.

▼ Sign Language. Spread abundant holiday cheer with an oversize greeting. Prime and then paint inexpensive plastic letters, purchased from a sign company, in shades of one color. Lay flowers or greens along the base of the greeting.

17

◀ Word Games. Let the kids have fun with a new take on a familiar game. Line up tiles from a Scrabble board game to form holiday phrases. Use them in a centerpiece, on an entryway table, or at place settings. Old wooden blocks and vintage printers' letters can be used similarly to create greetings.

fall festivities

Rich russets, toasty browns, and glowing golds bring warmth to autumn even on cool, crisp days. Bring those colors and intriguing textures to your table, doorway, or mantel by spreading the harvests of nature throughout your home.

Leaves so sheer that they resemble colorful shadows scatter across an autumn table. Called "leaf skeletons" because they show the veins and stems in see-through detail, they are made from leaves gathered from trees before they drop. Making the skeletons takes several weeks, so plan ahead. To allow for some leaves that will deteriorate beyond use as they process, make more than you plan to use.

making leaf skeletons

ᕫ Collect young, fresh leaves before they change color and drop. Leaves with the most pronounced veins work best.

Fill a container with water. Immerse the leaves in the water for two to four weeks or until the green leaf tissue softens. Change the water every few days, discarding leaves that become too soft. The longer the leaves are immersed, the easier it will be to remove the tissue.

Rinse the leaves under running water, lightly rubbing them until a transparent lacy skeleton remains. Place the leaves in a flower press or between unprinted newsprint and heavy books until they are dry and flattened.

Secure leaves to waxed paper with tape circles. Lightly spray them with gold, orange, or copper paint. Colors may be layered, one color misted over another. Coat the leaves as heavily as you wish. Flatten curled leaves between waxed paper and books for an hour.

table leaves

ᕫ Readymade or sewn from yardage, this canvas place mat displays a colorful leaf border. Arrange several leaves along one side of a place mat. Remove one leaf at a time and place it painted-side-down on waxed paper. Use a disposable foam brush to lightly apply tacky white crafts glue to the entire back surface of the leaf. Do not allow excess glue to puddle around the edges or veins. Replace the leaf and gently press it to the fabric. Repeat for additional leaves. When all the leaves are in place, cover the place mat with waxed paper and weight it with books. Let the glue dry for several hours, then peel away the waxed paper. To clean the place mat, gently wipe it with a damp cloth or spot-clean it as necessary.

tabletop pond

ॐ Puddles and ponds take on the look of an autumnal mosaic as leaves turn color and tumble. Echo that look on your table with one or more water-filled centerpieces. Layer a few brilliant leaves in the bottom of a shallow waterproof bowl or tray. Add water almost to the rim, then place a few floating candles in the dish.

leaf bags

ॐ Put guests in good favor with treat-filled bags set at each place. Purchase art-paper gift bags at party goods stores. Prepare leaf skeletons as described on *page 19*. Brush the back of the leaves with a thin coat of white crafts glue or apply spray adhesive. Press the leaf to the bag and smooth it with a piece of waxed paper. To hold the bag closed, cut two slits near the top, through both layers of the bag, and weave a twig through the slits. To make the place cards shown on *page 18*, glue a leaf to an art paper rectangle. Cut halfway around the leaf with a crafts knife, and fold the paper in half to make a tent. At the stem base, cut two slits to hold a twig. Insert a twig and write the guest's name below it.

20

autumn's glow

❧ Garnish plain pillar candles with semi-transparent leaves for an elegant and understated display. Tack leaf skeletons to the candles with a small circle of tape. Remove the leaves and tape one at a time and coat the backs of the leaves with decoupage medium. Smooth the leaves in place. If necessary, use tacky white crafts glue to hold the stems down. Cover the entire sides of the candle, including the leaves, with one or more coats of decoupage medium.

21

leaf napkin ring

❧ Deep colors of polymer clay and a bit of ribbon work into simple bead-like napkin rings. Knead the clay and form it into ¾×1×⅜-inch thick blocks. Using the shape shown at *left* as a guide, draw a leaf outline with veins, using a toothpick. Slide a thin wooden skewer through the bead at the horizontal center. Hang the skewer from the edges of a baking dish to elevate the bead. Bake the bead according to the clay manufacturer's directions. After cooling, coat the bead with varnish. Run ribbon thorough the hole to tie the bead around a napkin.

fall greetings

An autumn garland hung over the door allows guests and passersby to anticipate the atmosphere within. Magnolia branches, whether clipped from the yard or ordered from a florist, form the base. As they age, they take on a rich bronze color. Look for branches that naturally curve in the shape that best fits your doorway. We added orange silk leaves and berries, seeded eucalyptus, pheasant feathers, pinecones, and wire-edge ribbon; other items can be used just as successfully. Reserve a few items and make a matching swag to hang on the door. Drape the garland from a light fixture as shown, or insert small hooks in the door frame to hold the branches.

here's how...

Form the base. Clip magnolia or other sturdy, curving branches for the base and lay them out into the desired shape and fullness. Wire two or more branches together with medium-gauge floral wire, overlapping the stems of one section with the leaves of the next to cover the stems and wires.

Add the color. Wire long stems of silk leaves and branches of berries over the base. Hang and shape the garland. Tuck in seeded eucalyptus and pheasant feathers. Wire pinecones to the stems. As an option, weave a coordinating wire-edge ribbon through the garland.

beautiful bounty

Unexpected combinations often create the most interest. Elegant roses in a plain wooden basket, a rich tapestry that anchors weathered antlers, and a farmer's market pumpkin combined with simple taper candles create the juxtaposition that causes people to pause and take notice. A mirror propped in the background intensifies the display, adding brightness to the harvest colors. For the floral arrangement, line a wooden basket with a plastic container or several heavy plastic bags. Fill the container with dampened floral foam trimmed to fit the container. Insert peach and orange single-stem and spray roses in a rounded shape. Fill in the arrangement with seeded eucalyptus and hypericum (coffeebean berry or St.-John's-wort). As the materials dry and diminish in size, insert fresh items.

Trees both large and small pull a room together when their decorations and colors complement the rest of the decor.

well-trimmed

trees

Evergreens loaded with childhood ornaments and family vacation mementos never go out of style—or far from your heart. When decorating a grand tree in the main entertaining spot or even a tiny tabletop version in the entry, consider matching the tree decorations to the room. Pulling colors, textures, shapes, and motifs from the room brings everything together stunningly. The tree becomes part of the overall theme rather than a lone ornament that assumes its place for a few weeks.

it makes scents

ᴥ Bring sweet aromas into your home with a tree that looks as warm and spicy as it smells. Dried citrus slices, shimmering like stained glass, and star anise ornaments are reminders that two of the first holy gifts, frankincense and myrrh, also were fragrant.

To echo the lights of the season, a shining star tops the tree and candles,

made from dowels and copper, recalling old-fashioned candle-lit trees.

To dry orange slices, cut fresh oranges into ¼-inch-thick slices. Place them on a rack and set the rack in a cool, dry place with good air circulation. Let the slices dry for two or more weeks, turning them every few days. Orange slices also can be dried in commercial food dryers or on the lowest temperature in the oven. Purchased orange slices are available but may need to be brightened with floral spray paint. Pierce the slice and thread it onto an 18-inch length of ribbon, leaving long tails.

For the anise stars, trace around a saucer on quilting template plastic. Cut out the circle with decorative-edge scissors and punch a hole at the top for hanging. Hot-glue star anise to the shape.

The dowel candles are made from 3- to 5-inch pieces of ½-inch dowel. Paint the dowel white. Cut 1-inch-high flame shapes from 36-gauge copper foil. Tap a brad into the dowel top and glue the flame to the brad with epoxy or hot glue. Attach the candle to the tree with a Christmas tree candleholder clip (available where vintage-style Christmas ornaments are sold).

have a ball

∿ There's no need for a picnic table to look lonely and forlorn all winter long. Dress it in outdoor elements—snowmen, icicles, and snowball ornaments. For the snowmen, purchase wood cutouts or cut your own from thin Baltic birch plywood. Drill small holes at the tops and add wire for hanging. Cut a toothpick ¾-inch long for the nose. Drill a small hole in one snowman to receive the nose. Paint the snowmen white and the nose orange. Let the paint dry. "Frost" the snowmen with texture paste, available at crafts stores. While the paste is wet, sprinkle it with white glitter. Glue on beads for the eyes, mouth, and buttons. Glue the nose in place. For the snowballs, make a small hole in a plastic foam ball with a pencil. Glue both ends of an 8-inch strip of ribbon into the hole for a hanger. Coat the ball with texture paste and sprinkle the wet paste with white glitter.

26

it's the berries

Strawberry ornaments and peppermint-stripe ribbon whet the appetite for holiday festivities beyond the entryway. Reproductions of fruit ornaments similar to those that may have graced Grandma's tree are in keeping with the vintage bowls, cupboard, blanket, and painting. Traditional reds and greens maintain subtle holiday color when mixed with neutral colors and rustic textures. A bowl of fresh, velvet, beaded, or artificial strawberries expands the vintage fruit theme. If berries don't suit your taste, consider other single-theme decorations, such as candy canes, stars and stripes, or birds.

singing the blues

✍ A collection of flow-blue china and the rosy colors used to highlight it inspired this room as well as the decorated tree, which is just a couple steps shy of formal. Double bows of sheer gold-and-blue-plaid ribbon dangle ornaments from their centers. The juxtaposition of the formal sheer ribbon with the homespun plaid reflects the attitude of the room: well-appointed yet comfortable. Cobalt blue and silver mercury glass ornaments further echo the homeowner's display of blue-and-white china. Dried hydrangeas contribute to the naturalness of the paperwhite narcissus that fill the room and prevent the tree from looking too frou-frou.

In a Twinkling
ornaments

Keyed Up. Cardboard key tags make the perfect backing for miniature gem-covered ornaments. Remove the hanger and cover the tag with glitter glue. Press a flat marble or gem in the center. Wrap a strand of sequins (available at sewing and costume stores) around the center gem and press it into the glue. After the glue dries, attach a hanging ribbon.

Ribbon Candy. Gentle loops of ribbon and a few beads bring back memories of old-fashioned holiday candy. Cut a 22-inch length of ribbon. Thread several beads for the bottom dangle, looping the thread around the bottom bead to secure it. Form the ribbon into loops and stitch through the center of each loop, adding one or two beads with each stitch. End with a circle of ribbon. String small beads onto the thread for a hanging loop and knot the thread on the inside of the ribbon circle.

▶ Jingle Balls. A cluster of jingle bells rings with joy. Drill or punch a small hole in a 1½-inch diameter wooden ball and insert a screw eye. Spray-paint the ball metallic red. Hot-glue 12 mm jingle bells over the ball, packing them tightly. Spray the bells red, using several light coats of paint. Attach a ribbon through the screw eye.

◀ Message in a Bauble. Place holiday wishes in transparent glass ornaments for sentiments that float like bubbles. Cut phrases from old cards or print them on your computer. Trim the paper, leaving a margin at one end. Insert the strip into the ball and replace the cap, catching the margin in the cap to hold the strip. If necessary, hot-glue the cap in place.

31

▶ Pretty Prisms. Trees twinkle with the elegance of a chandelier when beads and prisms dangle from the branches. Knot silver embroidery thread around a ½-inch diameter jump ring. Thread the cord through several ½- to ¾-inch beads and loop it through the hanger at the top of a 4-inch prism. Slide the thread back through the beads and tie it to the jump ring. Secure the knot with a dot of glue.

Sock it to 'em with stockings made from fun materials and designed with special people and their interests in mind.

stockings *for all*

Generic stockings fill store shelves during the holidays. A stocking created with one person or an entire family in mind, however, comes from the heart. Start with a basic commercial pattern or our general instructions to sew stockings such as those on *pages 34–36*. Modify shapes and sizes to suit your wishes, mantel size, or the gifts you'll tuck inside. Shop for unexpected materials that express personality, including novelty fabrics. Embellish the stockings with trims and sparkles to complete the package.

basic stocking assembly instructions

To create the stocking shape, use a commercial stocking pattern, trace an old stocking, or draw your own. Modify the shape to fit your preference and the material you will use. Add seam allowances where needed.

For lined stockings, cut two stocking fronts and two stocking backs. If desired, cut a layer of lightweight batting to add softness and loft. For unlined stockings, cut one front and one back. For lightweight or stretchy fabrics, baste or fuse interfacing to the wrong side of fabric. Cut out the stocking shapes, reversing the pattern to make fronts and backs. Embellish the stocking before sewing the front and back together.

Sew the stocking front to the back, leaving the top open. Clip the curves and turn the stocking right side out. Sew the stocking lining in the same manner, leaving an opening for turning along one long side.

Cut a cuff to fit around the top. For a straight cuff, cut it double the desired finished depth to form a self lining. For a shaped cuff, cut a separate lining piece. With right sides together, sew the lining to the cuff along the shaped edge. For either cuff, sew the short ends together to form a fabric circle. Turn the cuff, wrong sides facing and raw edges matching, and press the lower edge in place.

For an unlined stocking, slip the cuff inside the stocking, wrong side of the cuff facing the wrong side of the stocking, and aligning the tops. Sew the cuff to the stocking around the upper edge. Fold the cuff over the stocking, encasing the raw edges.

For a lined stocking, slip the cuff over the outside of the stocking, wrong side of the cuff facing the right side of the stocking, and aligning the tops. Baste the cuff to the stocking around the upper edge.

Slip the stocking into the lining, right sides facing. Sew around the upper cuff edge. Turn the stocking right side out through the opening in the lining. Slip-stich the opening closed. Slide the lining into the stocking and fold the cuff down over the top.

ripple effect

Cardboard stockings take the place of gift bags and double as door greetings at the home of an avid gardener. For each stocking, cut two shapes from corrugated or embossed cardboard found at arts and crafts stores. Cut and overlay a cuff shape on the front of one stocking, if desired. Punch holes along the lengths, and lace the two pieces together with leather strips or boot laces. Knot the ends and attach a second lace for hanging.

simple
elegance

∾ Satin, velvet, and sheer ribbon are combined in Victorian, heirloom-style stockings. Solid, monochromatic fabrics allow the embellishments to shine.

For the blue beaded stocking, draw curves and spirals on the stocking front, then couch strands of beads over the lines before assembly. To couch, take a small hand stitch between beads, spacing stitches an inch or less apart.

Sewn-on beads make the purple stocking sparkle. Strands of larger beads dangle from the cuff points.

To quilt the fabric for the green stocking, cut satin, lightweight batting, and tear-away stabilizer larger than the pattern. Draw a diamond grid onto the tear-away stabilizer. Layer the fabric, batting, and stabilizer and follow the manufacturer's directions to machine-quilt along the grid lines.

Note: Follow the basic stocking assembly instructions on *page 32* to complete the stockings.

35

for the oui ones

Crisp fabrics, wiggly rickrack trim, and prints inspired by the pages of favorite French children's stories make kids say "oo la la" on Christmas morn. Match stockings to the interests of each child by perusing novelty fabrics in sewing center aisles. You'll find prints that depict sports, favorite foods, toys, action figures, athletic teams, cartoon and television characters, and just about any other interest your child may have.

screen stars

Classic shapes take on arty, industrial design when made from aluminum window screen. When working with screen, wear protective eyewear when cutting and wear work gloves while handling to protect against metal fragments and rough edges. Cut stocking pairs from screening material with utility scissors, allowing extra length for cuffs. Leaving the top edge open, whipstitch stockings together with a large-eye needle and fine silver wire. Turn down a cuff and press it in place with gloved fingers. Hand-sew trim to the cuff edge or attach charms or strands of beads to the cuff with large jump rings. Look for charms in jewelry-making sections of crafts stores to match individual interests. **Note:** Keep screen stockings away from small children as the edges will be scratchy.

37

No beauty is greater than that of nature itself. Bring the grace of the outdoors to your home in refreshing ways this holiday season.

natural
elegance

There are no substitutes for the colors and textures that both fresh and dried natural materials bring into an arrangement. Soft heather, dried herbs, pinecones and pods of all shapes and sizes, even seeds, become as important as traditional greenery and ribbons. Their ability to last often spans more than the few weeks during Christmas.

heather tree and wreath

Soft heather offers a variation on the theme of a tabletop evergreen tree. Wedge pieces of damp floral foam into a small bucket, foam extending ½ inch beyond the top of the bucket. Starting at the center with the tallest stems, insert heather into the foam. Work outward, creating a tree shape. Add sprigs of variegated mini pittosporum or ivy around the base to cover the foam. Tie a large matching bow around the bucket.

For the wreath, wire small sprigs of heather into clusters using floral wire. Insert the clusters into a grapevine wreath base. Cover each preceding cluster end with the cluster just added, working in one direction for an uninterrupted shape. Attach a soft, sheer bow. As the heather dries, it will shrink slightly. Make and set aside a few extra heather clusters to insert into bare spots as needed.

pinecone bobeches

here's how...

Do it to scales. Interlock the scales of small pinecones to create a collar around a candlestick. Choose a candlestick with a built-in bobeche. Slip the scales of a pinecone over the bobeche and hot-glue them in place, repeating to completely encircle with pinecones.

Go for the gold. Add a bit of sparkle by gluing tiny gold beads to the pinecones. Use a small glue gun to place a dot of glue on a scale. Lay the bead in place with bent-nose tweezers or pliers.

pinecone and nut wreath

Dress the bathroom with a wreath that encircles pretty toiletries. Fit a twig wreath to a stool, plate, or platter, ensuring that the center opening is large enough to hold soaps, lotions, or other items. Hot-glue small pinecones (available at crafts and floral supply stores) to the wreath to almost cover. Add a variety of nuts, gluing them in place over the pinecones and in any empty spaces. To add bits of color to match the room, add small colored pebbles, shells, feathers, or other accents. Attach a wide sheer ribbon and tie it in a simple knot.

43

pantry candles

 Dried beans and peas give pebbly texture to pillar candles. Cut sheets of beeswax to fit plain pillar candles. Warm the beeswax with a hair dryer and press it to the candles. Warm the beeswax again and roll the candle in dried bean mix, dried peas, or other legumes. Tie a strip of raffia around each candle.

Run a piece of dried corn husk (available at crafts stores) through a paper crimper. Fold the husk in half crosswise and cut it to size. Slip the husk under the raffia.

For the wax medallions, melt sealing wax onto waxed paper according to the manufacturer's instructions. Stamp the warm wax with a seal. After the medallion cools, glue it to the candle.

seeds of inspiration

 Go nutty with a bowl filled with natural orbs. Cover plastic foam balls with a variety of nuts and dried beans. Seeds, feathers, shells, and small pinecones work equally well and are attached in the same manner.

Place a plastic foam ball on a cup or container to keep it from rolling. Using a low-temperature hot-glue gun, glue the nuts or beans to the ball. For oval items, glue one tip to the ball and one tip pointing outward, allowing the items to be packed tightly together. To cover with flat nuts, overlap them to keep the base of the ball concealed, using tweezers or needle nose pliers if necessary. Let the glue dry and rotate the ball to glue items to the remaining side to cover it completely. Fill in with additional nuts or beans, keeping the shape as round as possible.

pinecone trees

ᴗ If you yearn for an urn or pine for a tiny topiary, combine those two wishes into one quick-and-easy project. Fit a long, narrow pinecone into a small metal or ceramic urn for a tabletop tree.

Cut floral foam to fit the urn, trim it 1 inch below the top of the urn, and wedge or hot-glue it in place. Press the base of a large pinecone into the floral foam to make an indentation. Hot-glue the pinecone into the floral foam and hold it steady until the glue cools. Glue around the edges, if necessary, to stabilize the pinecone.

Insert small sprigs of greenery into the floral foam at the base, covering the foam. Insert small clusters of wired berries into the foam. Hot-glue nuts, seed pods, or other dried materials to the greens.

herb topiaries

ᴗ These little trees make lots of scents. Covering a plastic foam cone with your favorite herb is a great way to add subtle fragrance to any room. Consider lavender for the bathroom or bedroom, parsley or rosemary for the kitchen, or crushed dried mint leaves for a powder room.

Paint a small clay pot as desired. Cut floral foam to fit the pot and hot-glue it in place. Cover a small plastic foam cone with tacky crafts glue and roll the cone in dried herbs to completely cover it. Use a long cinnamon stick to join the base of the cone to the floral foam in the pot and glue it in place. Cover the top of the floral foam with deer moss. Glue a small painted ball, finial, or ornament to the top.

The seven days between Christmas and New Year's are a time of reflection and sharing for many African-American families.

kwanza
celebration

From December 26 to January 1, many African-Americans celebrate their heritage and traditions. The observance of Kwanza, begun in 1966, does not replace the observances of Christmas or Hanukkah. Rather, the time is used to focus on the seven principles of the African culture: umoja (unity), kujichagulia (self-determination), ujima (collective work and responsibility), ujamaa (cooperative economics), nia (purpose), kuumba (creativity), and imani (faith).

The colors used during the holiday represent African-American history: green for the fertile lands of Africa, black for the color of the people, and red for the blood shed in the struggle for freedom. Gift-giving is a modest part of the celebration and it is essential that gifts be educational or handmade.

Seven candles are arranged, shown *opposite,* with three red on the right, three green on the left, and one black in the center. Each has a tag with one of the seven principles attached, and every night a candle is lit. A kinara (candleholder) often is used to display Kwanza candles. Fruits, vegetables, and nuts, an ear of corn for each child, a unity cup, and African mats or cloths are incorporated into decorations.

kwanza gift display

An arrangement of traditional gifts is ready to share with friends and family who may stop by. Mesh bags filled with papayas, mangoes, blood oranges, pineapples, kiwi fruits, plantains, raw peanuts, and sugar cane can be placed in plain or hand-painted wooden bowls, baskets, or simply arranged in mesh bags. To make bags, buy lengths of mesh tubing at crafts stores and cut it to the approximate length. Knot one end and turn the tubing inside out, knot to the inside. Fill the bags with food gifts and tie the top with raffia and eucalyptus stems. Place the bags on an African batik (a mud cloth or woven mat work equally well) and place a pitcher or unity cup and other African arts and crafts in the arrangement.

Take one tree-lot wreath, add items that match your home or holiday decor, and you have an elegant seasonal greeting.

There's no need to start from scratch when making a holiday wreath. Buy a good-quality mixed-green wreath and embellish it to suit your taste. We'll show you the basics, then you can use your imagination.

personal
wreaths

fruits and feathers

here's how...

1 Establish a base. Fit a ring over the center of the wreath. Various sizes of metal rings are available in the floral and general crafts sections of arts and crafts stores.

2 Add grape clusters. Wire beaded grape clusters to the ring, stems extending inward, and leaving room between clusters for an apple ornament.

3 Pin the ring in place. Bend floral wire into a hairpin shape. Put the ring in place and slide a pin over it between each set of grapes. Twist the wire at the back of the wreath to hold the ring.

4 Attach the apples. Squeeze a puddle of hot glue between each grape cluster and over the wire. Press a beaded apple into the glue, one apple at a time, and hold it until the glue cools.

5 Finish with feathers. Slide the tips of peacock feathers among the greenery. Lift the foliage and use a dot of hot glue to hold the feathers in place.

stars and squiggles

✎ Add sparkle and fun to a wreath with purchased star ornaments and narrow wire-edge ribbon or wired beads. Cluster stars on one quadrant of a wreath. For interest, use at least two different styles of stars but keep them similar in color, material, and style. Wind narrow wire-edge ribbon or wired beads around various sizes of dowels, broom handles, and other items. Uncurl the ribbons or beads and tuck them into the greenery. Use a small dab of hot glue to hold the ends in place.

golden oak wreath

here's how...

1 Establish a base. Fit a ring over the center of the wreath. Various sizes of metal rings are available in the floral and general crafts sections of arts and crafts stores.

2 Make a stem. Trim a small wire-end silk leaf (available in the bridal area of stores) to fit behind a purchased preserved oak leaf. Press the preserved oak leaves with an iron to lie flat.

3 Attach the wires. Apply hot glue to a trimmed silk leaf. Glue a silk leaf to the back of each pressed oak leaf, creating a wire stem to attach the leaves to the metal ring.

4 Attach the leaves. Wrap the wire stems around the metal ring, slightly overlapping the leaves. When the ring is full, paint both sides of the ring and leaves with copper metallic spray paint.

5 Secure the ring. Bend floral wire into a hairpin shape. Position the ring. Slide the pins over the ring, spaced about 4 inches apart. Twist the wire at the back of the wreath to hold the ring.

6 Finishing touches. Hot-glue various sizes and finishes of gold balls to the ring, ornament caps toward the greens. Wire a burlap bow to the wreath.

Interwoven colors of reds and greens create an intermingling of memories at this most special time of year.

mad about *plaid*

There's something about plaid that makes winters warmer, homes cozier, and attitudes more relaxed. Maybe it's the hint of wooly scarves and flannel shirts, memories of curling up in a multicolored blanket after a cold day of sledding, or the sight of bright ribbons that wind around packages and wreaths. Whatever the reason, plaid is one of the staples of the holiday season.

The rag-ball-style plaid ribbon ornaments on the homespun tree shown *opposite* determine the colors for the tree's other decorations: a twig garland wound with red and green raffia, brown paper cones filled to the brim with glossy pepperberries, wooden animal shapes cut from cookie-cutter patterns and painted barn red, and a cardboard star sporting a sprig of greenery and more pepperberries. Under the tree, plaids abound in ribbons wrapped around kraft-paper packages and baskets of homemade goodies. Although at least a half-dozen different plaids reside on or under the tree, they get along well because of the common colors and scale.

grapevine garland

here's how...

Wrap it up. Loosely wrap purchased grapevine garland with continuous strands of red and green raffia. Grapevine garland often comes tightly wound like a wreath. Unwind it and let it rest a few days to allow it to drape easily. To join two garlands, overlap and intertwine the ends.

Wrap 12-inch wires around the upper scales of pinecones. Sort pinecones into clusters of three and twist the wires into a stem. Prepare enough clusters to space them 12 inches apart on the garland.

Add the trims. Divide caspia into small bundles and wire the stems together. Attach the pinecone clusters to the garland approximately every 12 inches. Slide the caspia bundles and small bunches of pepperberries under the raffia, lacing the stems into the grapevine. Dot with hot glue as needed.

fleece and plaid stockings

These stockings are the cat's meow in a family of feline lovers, but they'd be equally at home with only family names attached. Make the stockings following the instructions on *page 32* using fleece for the stocking, percale for the lining, and plaid wool for the cuff, heel, and toe. Cut the heel and toe following the outer pattern lines. Fuse the heel and toe to the fleece and add blanket stitches or other embroidery stitches as desired. Spell out names with wooden letters and glue the letters on the cuffs. Adorn the lower edge of each cuff with trim or self fringe. For added fun, dangle a cut-out ornament from a ribbon tacked beneath the cuff.

all-around plaid

Wrap it up. Wrap 3-, 4-, and 5-inch-diameter plastic foam balls with 1-inch-wide plaid ribbon or plaid fabric torn into 1-inch-wide strips. Secure the fabric with pins as you wrap. At the top of the ball, fold the ribbon end into a point and anchor it with a corsage pin.

Tie it on. Slide one or more beads onto another corsage pin and push the pin into the ball opposite the first pin. Slide ribbon or raffia under several strips of fabric at the top of the ball and tie it in a knot to form a hanging loop. Slide the knot under the fabric and pin it in place.

55

sleigh bell wreath

✺ Antique or reproduction sleigh bells remind everyone that Santa is on his way. Purchase a fresh evergreen wreath slightly smaller in diameter than the length of the bell strap. Wire the bells diagonally across the wreath, tucking the ends to the back and letting the strap buckle slightly. Wire a long cluster of pepperberries to the top of the wreath, tucking the ends under the bell strap. Tie a ribbon into a double bow with long tails and wire it over the stems and strap.

goody basket

✺ Few things are better than gifts from the heart—and the pantry. Fill baskets with homemade preserves and other treats. Customize baskets with favorite foods for special friends and make up a few extra packages for people who drop by or to use as hostess gifts. To give it a festive look, line the basket with a red-and-green plaid napkin or cloth, tie a ribbon on the handle, and tuck in greenery.

pepperberry cornucopia

57

Cut it out. Using decorative-edge scissors, cut an 8-inch-diameter circle from kraft paper. Mark the center of the circle. Cut a straight line from one edge to the center point with plain scissors.

On a roll. Twist the paper into a cone. Glue the edges in place using a low-temperature glue gun. Stuff the cone with tissue paper to just below the upper edge. Use dots of glue to hold the tissue paper in place. Glue the ends of a 10-inch ribbon to opposite sides of the top for a hanging loop.

Fill 'er up. Glue pepperberries to the tissue paper and along the edge of the cone. Mound the pepperberries over the top of the cone, allowing a few to drape over the sides.

Brown kraft paper, cut with decorative-edge scissors and rolled into a cornucopia, resembles old-fashioned soda fountain-variety ice cream cones. Here, pepperberries spill over the top. Other full-shape dried flowers and fresh greenery would work just as well for fillers and would give the cones a completely different look.

Getting Wired. Wrap a bit of heavy metal magic around pillar candles. Find flexible wires at crafts, hardware, and jewelry supply stores. Bend ½ inch at a right angle and pierce it into the candle. Wrap the wire around the candle. When the wrapping is complete, clip the wire and bend and pierce the last ½ inch into the candle.

In a Twinkling
candles

Tea Lights. Transform a plain tea cup into a sparkling votive holder. Place a tea light or small votive in a tea cup, keeping it level and away from the cup edges. Carefully fill the cup with marbles from a floral department.

Jar Candles. These country candles couldn't be faster or easier to make. Pack the bottom of a canning jar with greenery that has stiff leaves or needles (such as boxwood, holly, or fir). Place a handful of fresh cranberries on top. Add water to just below the rim of the jar. Cap it off with a floating candle.

▶ Citrus Shiners. Towers of lemons and limes add brightness to breakfast or brunch. Place small fruits in clear glass cylinders, then fill the vessels with water. Float brightly colored candles on the top. With a contemporary look on a plain platter, these fruit candles also could be a clean, crisp addition for a colonial setting.

◀ Leaf Votives. Salal leaves transform a plain votive holder into an elegant little light. Clip a leaf to a candle cup with a clothespin. Hot-glue a second leaf to the first, overlapping them and shaping them to the cup, adding leaves around the cup. Trim the lower edges even with the bottom. Tie a ribbon around the leaves.

59

▶ Icy Lights. It's a true combination of fire and ice. Melt clear candle wax according to the package directions. Center a plain taper candle in a clean milk carton. Pack the carton with ice, keeping the taper centered. Carefully pour the melted wax into the carton until only the wick of the taper is exposed. Let the candle cool undisturbed until solid, at least one hour. Pour out the water and carefully tear away the carton.

During the time that celebrates eight nights of light, brighten your home with a shimmering menorah, sweet-scented garlands, and candles that twinkle with symbols of faith.

bright and light
hanukkah

Scraps of colored and opalescent glass glimmer in a rich pattern on a mosaic menorah. To make one, look for glass scraps and special mosaic nippers at stained glass supply stores.

mosaic menorah

here's how...

Prepare the materials. Build a wooden base from an 18-inch-long piece of 2×4-inch lumber. Glue a smaller raised platform over the base and place a final block in the center for the shamus. Insert candle cups in the raised portions. Using glass cutters, nip glass into pieces about ½-inch square.

Glue the glass. Working on one side at a time, glue the glass to the boards. Use large dabs of mosaic glue (wood soaks up the glue), but not so much that the glass shifts. If desired, make a star shape in the center using triangular pieces. Place the glass squares close to the edges, and leave even spaces between them for grout. Let the glue dry.

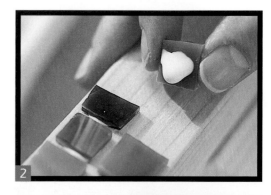

Apply the grout. Work non-sanded grout into all the spaces and along any exposed edges. Using a damp sponge, wipe away the excess grout. Rinse the sponge often. After the grout begins to dry, buff the glass to remove the hazy residue. Glue felt to the bottom of the menorah.

candle box

An unfinished jewelry box gets the stamp of approval as a container for Hanukkah candles. Paint the box with two or more coats of white paint. Using rubber stamps and blue ink, stamp blue stars on the sides and top of the box. Center the "Happy Hanukkah" stamped or written greeting on the lid. For the silver stars and menorahs, stamp a single image with silver ink. Pour silver embossing powder over the wet image. Tap off the excess powder and heat the powder with an embossing tool until it is smooth and shiny. Repeat for each silver image. Color the candles and flames with yellow and blue fabric markers.

spicy garland

Small symbols of Hanukkah fill the room with the aroma of warm spices. Mix one cup of applesauce with four ounces of cinnamon, one teaspoon of cloves, and half a teaspoon of nutmeg to form a stiff dough. Roll the dough ¼ inch thick and cut out shapes with cookie cutters. Use toothpicks to make dots and other decorations, and use a straw to pierce a hole for hanging. Place the ornaments on a rack and let them dry for at least two weeks, turning them every few days. When they are dry, string the ornaments on a garland or tie them to gifts. Wrap them in tissue for yearly storage or crumble them into your Havdalah spice box.

star of david candle

❧ Silver eyelets from the notions department of a sewing store form a contemporary Star of David design on a blue pillar candle. Cut tissue paper to fit the side of the candle and draw a Star of David onto paper for a pattern. Tape the pattern to the candle and transfer the design to the candle by tracing over it with a pencil, lightly inscribing the candle with the star. Beginning at the points of the star and working inward, center eyelets over the lines, placing them close together to conceal the lines. Carefully push eyelets into the candle. A 4×4-inch candle with a 3½×3¾-inch star will require about 60 eyelets.

The Holidays bring many special days for families to celebrate, with togetherness at the heart of the season. When people gather, and favorite foods are served—when the recipes are right and the fires warm—hearts open and conversations flow. These will be the fond memories of future gatherings, the recipes becoming the one element that bridges them. Here is a rich collection of old favorites and fresh creations to make every holiday gathering a celebration for reminiscing and tradition sharing.

GATHERI

NGtogether

Orange- and Herb-Roasted Turkey
(see recipe, page 68)

66

Showcasing citrus, cranberries, chestnuts, pears, pumpkin, root vegetables, and other favorite seasonal flavors, this menu, perfect for Thanksgiving or Christmas, takes advantage of winter's blessed bounty.

feasting *on the* season's flavors

It's true—with today's wide-reaching food networks, you usually can find raspberries in December and acorn squash in July. But contemporary American bistro chefs have taught us what Old World chefs have known all along: Food tastes best when menus march to the cadences of each season's bounty. It's why we crave root vegetables in winter and rhubarb in spring. So while summer's homegrown tomatoes are but a distant memory by the time the holidays roll around, November and December's produce aisles are brimming with equally cherished foods that are at their freshest, in-season best right now. These are the flavors celebrated in this festive menu.

winter-fresh menu

Fig and Prosciutto Pâté

✳

Chestnut and Parsnip Soup

✳

Orange- and Herb-Roasted Turkey

✳

Mashed Turnips and Sweets

✳

Herbed Leek Gratin

✳

Layered Cranberry-Apple Mold

✳

Spiced Pears and Camembert

✳

Country Pumpkin Torte

✳

BEFORE THE HOLIDAY:

up to 3 months ahead:
■ Prepare cake for Country Pumpkin Torte; do not frost layers. Place cooled cake layers on a baking sheet; freeze until firm. Wrap and seal in moisture- and vapor-proof wrap or place in freezer bags and freeze up to 3 months.

up to 1 week ahead:
■ Prepare Candied Orange Peel for Country Pumpkin Torte. Store the peel, tightly covered, in a cool, dry place for up to 1 week. Or freeze up to 6 months.

several days ahead:
■ If using a frozen turkey, thaw in the refrigerator, allowing one day for every 5 pounds.

up to 2 days ahead:
■ Prepare Chestnut and Parsnip Soup through pureeing step; transfer to small shallow containers. Cover and chill.

up to 24 hours ahead:
■ Prepare Mashed Turnips and Sweets according to make-ahead directions, page 72.
■ Poach pears for Spiced Pears and Camembert; cover and chill.
■ Prepare Layered Cranberry-Apple Mold. Cover and chill.
■ Prepare Fig and Prosciutto Pâté.
■ Prepare Cream Cheese Frosting for the Country Pumpkin Torte; cover and chill.

DAY OF CELEBRATION:

4 to 5 hours ahead:
■ Begin roasting turkey; follow directions for roasting, cutting band of skin between drumsticks, uncovering, and standing.
■ Thaw Country Pumpkin Torte cakes at room temperature; when thawed, assemble as directed. Cover and chill.

1 to 2 hours ahead:
■ Prepare Herbed Leek Gratin.

approximately 30 minutes ahead:
■ Reheat Mashed Turnips and Sweets as directed; make accompanying relish.

just before serving:
■ Unmold Fig and Prosciutto Pâté.
■ Reheat Chestnut and Parsnip Soup, adding the half-and-half and garnishing as directed.
■ Unmold Layered Cranberry-Apple Mold.
■ Before main course is served, allow Camembert for Spiced Pears and Camembert to come to room temperature. (Serve pears as desired: To serve pears slightly warm, gently reheat over low heat before serving. To serve at room temperature, allow to stand while main course is served. You also can serve the pears chilled.)

30 minutes before dessert:
■ Let Country Pumpkin Torte stand, covered, at room temperature.

Orange- and Herb-Roasted Turkey

✳

This bird gets extra spark with a burst of orange—one of the freshest flavors of winter. Bring it to the table bedecked in candied fruits (also known as glacé), found in specialty food shops.

1   14-pound turkey
    Salt
    Freshly ground black pepper
1   medium onion, cut into wedges
1   medium orange, cut into wedges
6   fresh rosemary sprigs
    (4 to 5 inches long)
4   fresh thyme sprigs
    (4 to 5 inches long)
1   to 2 tablespoons cooking oil
1   6-ounce can frozen orange
    juice concentrate, thawed
¾   cup reduced-sodium chicken
    broth
¼   cup butter or margarine, melted
    Reduced-sodium chicken broth
4   teaspoons finely snipped fresh
    rosemary or 2 teaspoons
    dried rosemary, crushed
3   tablespoons cornstarch
¼   cup reduced-sodium chicken
    broth
    Candied fruit slices and/or fresh
    fruit, such as pears, oranges,
    and kumquats (optional)

Preheat oven to 325°F. Season cavity generously with salt and pepper. Place onion and orange wedges in cavity along with rosemary sprigs and thyme sprigs.
Pull turkey neck skin to back; fasten with skewer. If a band of skin crosses the tail, tuck drumsticks under the band. If there is no band, tie drumsticks securely to tail. Twist wing tips under the back.
Place bird, breast side up, on rack in a shallow roasting pan. Brush skin lightly with oil. Insert a meat thermometer into center of one of the inside thigh muscles, but not touching bone. Cover bird loosely with foil, leaving air space between bird and foil. Roast in the

preheated oven about 3¾ hours total: After 2½ hours, cut band of skin or string between drumsticks so thighs will cook evenly. Continue to roast, covered with foil, about 20 minutes more or until thermometer registers 160°F.

Stir together orange juice concentrate, the ¾ cup chicken broth, and the melted butter or margarine. Remove foil; brush some of the orange mixture over bird. Continue roasting, uncovered, until meat thermometer registers 180°F, brushing some of the remaining orange mixture over bird every 15 minutes. Reserve any remaining orange mixture for gravy. (When bird is done, the drumsticks should move easily in their sockets and the thickest parts of the drumsticks should be very soft when pressed.)

Remove turkey from oven and discard ingredients from cavity. Transfer turkey to a platter and let stand, covered with foil to keep warm, for 15 to 20 minutes before carving.

Meanwhile, to make the gravy, strain juices from roasting pan into a large glass measure. (Also scrape the browned bits into the cup.) Skim off and discard fat. Add the remaining orange mixture to juices in measuring cup. Measure liquid and add additional chicken broth, if necessary, to equal 3 cups. Pour juices into a medium saucepan. Add snipped or crushed rosemary. Combine cornstarch and the ¼ cup chicken broth. Add to saucepan. Cook and stir over medium heat until thickened and bubbly; cook and stir for 2 minutes more. Season to taste with additional salt and pepper. Remove from heat.

Just before serving, garnish platter with candied fruit slices and/or fresh fruit, if desired. Pass gravy with turkey. Makes 10 to 12 servings.

Nutrition facts per serving: 469 cal., 23 g total fat (8 g sat. fat), 185 mg chol., 261 mg sodium, 10 g carbo., 0 g fiber, 52 g pro.

Fig and Prosciutto Pâté

69

Fig and Prosciutto Pâté

✳

As soon as dried figs start appearing in the produce aisle around the holidays, snap some up for this luscious spread. Pair with pears for a doubly seasonal treat.

- 1 8-ounce container mascarpone cheese
- 2 ounces prosciutto, finely chopped
- ¼ cup finely chopped dried figs
- ¼ cup finely chopped walnuts, toasted
- 1 3-ounce package cream cheese, softened
  Kumquat wedges (optional)
  Fresh savory (optional)
  Pear or apple slices, strawberries, or other fresh fruit

Combine mascarpone cheese, prosciutto, figs, and nuts in a medium mixing bowl. Line a small bowl (1½-cup capacity) or crock with plastic wrap. Pack cheese mixture into the lined container; smooth top. Cover and chill for 2 to 24 hours.

To serve, lift cheese mold out of bowl. Remove plastic wrap. Spread softened cream cheese over mold. Allow to stand at room temperature for 20 to 30 minutes before serving. Garnish plate with kumquat wedges and fresh savory, if desired. Serve with fresh fruit. Store leftovers, covered, in the refrigerator up to 3 days. Makes 14 to 16 servings.

Nutrition facts per serving: 144 cal., 11 g total fat (6 g sat. fat), 30 mg chol., 142 mg sodium, 9 g carbo., 1 g fiber, 6 g pro.

Herbed Leek Gratin

✳

Line up the slender, tender leek halves in an au gratin dish, then add a creamy marjoram sauce and cheese-flecked crumb topping.

4 pounds thin leeks
⅔ cup whipping cream
⅔ cup chicken broth
½ teaspoon freshly ground black pepper
¼ cup snipped fresh marjoram or 2 tablespoons snipped fresh thyme
2 cups fresh French or Italian bread crumbs
¼ cup grated Parmesan cheese
¼ cup butter, melted
Fresh marjoram sprigs (optional)

Preheat oven to 425°F. Generously butter a 2- to 2½- quart au gratin dish or rectangular baking dish. Trim roots off leeks, leaving pieces 4 to 5 inches long with white and pale green parts. Cut the leeks in half lengthwise and rinse thoroughly under running cold water; pat dry. Arrange leeks, cut side down, in the baking dish, overlapping as necessary to fit.

Combine the whipping cream and chicken broth; pour over the leeks. Sprinkle with pepper and half of the snipped herb. Cover the dish tightly with foil and bake in the preheated oven 20 minutes.

Meanwhile, combine the bread crumbs, Parmesan cheese, melted butter, and remaining snipped herb in a small bowl. Uncover leeks and sprinkle with bread crumb mixture. Bake, uncovered, 10 to 15 minutes more or until leeks are tender and crumbs are golden brown. If desired, garnish with fresh marjoram sprigs. Makes 8 servings.

Note: If cooking this recipe with Orange- and Herb-Roasted Turkey, cook the gratin, covered, for 55 minutes at 325°F. When turkey comes out of oven to stand, increase oven temperature to 425°F. Sprinkle with crumb mixture and bake the gratin, uncovered, for 10 to 15 minutes more or until leeks are tender and crumbs are golden brown.

Nutrition facts per serving: 216 cal., 15 g total fat (9 g sat. fat), 46 mg chol., 275 mg sodium, 17 g carbo., 2 g fiber, 4 g pro.

Herbed Leek Gratin

Layered Cranberry-Apple Mold

Layered Cranberry-Apple Mold

✳

- 1 6-ounce package lemon-
  flavored gelatin
- ½ cup sugar
- 1 cup boiling water
- 1½ cups cranberry-apple drink
- 1 16-ounce can whole cranberry
  sauce
- 1 1.3-ounce envelope dessert
  topping mix
- 1 large unpeeled apple, cored
  and finely chopped (1¼ cups)
- ¼ cup mayonnaise or salad dressing
  Sugared cranberries* (optional)
  Fresh mint (optional)

Dissolve gelatin and sugar in the boiling water. Stir in cranberry-apple drink. Transfer 1¾ cups of the mixture to another bowl; cover and chill about 30 minutes or until partially set (the consistency of egg whites). Set remaining gelatin-drink mixture aside.
Fold cranberry sauce into partially set gelatin-drink mixture; pour into an 8-cup ring mold or a 2-quart square dish. Cover and chill about 30 minutes or until almost firm. Chill remaining gelatin-drink mixture about 30 minutes or until partially set (the consistency of egg whites).
Meanwhile, prepare topping mix according to package directions; fold into partially set gelatin-drink mixture along with apple and mayonnaise. Spoon over chilled cranberry sauce-gelatin layer in mold or dish.
Cover and chill about 6 hours or until firm. Unmold gelatin onto platter. (For easier unmolding, set mold into a sink filled with warm water for several seconds or until gelatin separates from the mold.) If desired, garnish with sugared cranberries and mint. Serves 12.
*Note: For sugared cranberries, freeze cranberries; roll in sugar until coated.

Nutrition facts per serving: 222 cal., 5 g total fat (2 g sat. fat), 2 mg chol., 95 mg sodium, 44 g carbo., 1 g fiber, 2 g pro.

Chestnut and Parsnip Soup

✳

Enjoy an elegant first course featuring the once-a-year treat of fresh chestnuts.

- 1 tablespoon walnut oil or
  cooking oil
- 1 pound parsnips, peeled and
  chopped (about 3½ cups)
- 2 cups shelled roasted chestnuts*
  or one 10-ounce can whole
  chestnuts packed in water,
  drained
- 1 medium onion, chopped (½ cup)
- 2 cloves garlic, minced
- ⅛ teaspoon ground white pepper
- 3 14-ounce cans reduced-sodium
  chicken broth
- 3 sprigs fresh marjoram
- 1 cup half-and-half or light cream

Heat oil in a large saucepan. Add parsnips, chestnuts, onion, garlic, and pepper. Cover; cook over medium heat 10 minutes or until parsnips are tender, stirring often. Add broth and bring to boiling; reduce heat. Simmer, uncovered, for 20 minutes. Add marjoram; cook for 10 minutes more. Remove marjoram; discard. Cool soup slightly.

Place one-third of mixture in a blender container. Cover; blend until smooth (cover blender with a clean towel while operating). Return mixture to a clean saucepan. Repeat with remaining soup. Stir in ½ cup of the half-and-half; heat through. Ladle into bowls. Swirl remaining half-and-half into each serving. Makes 7 cups (10 to 12 side-dish servings).
*Note: To roast chestnuts, use the tip of a sturdy paring knife to carefully cut an "X" on the flat side of each chestnut. Place in a shallow baking pan and roast in a 400°F oven for 15 minutes or until corners of Xs curl up. Peel while warm; remove papery skin by rolling peeled chestnuts in a towel. Three and one-quarter cups unshelled chestnuts will yield about 2 cups shelled. Whole, fresh chestnuts are available from November to January. They will keep for up to two weeks in the refrigerator, or several months in the freezer, in an airtight container. You also can find them canned or dried in many supermarkets.

Nutrition facts per serving: 169 cal., 5 g total fat (2 g sat. fat), 9 mg chol., 324 mg sodium, 28 g carbo., 4 g fiber, 4 g pro.

Spiced Pears and Camembert

72

Mashed Turnips and Sweets

✳

It's great to know you can get a head start on this autumn-inspired recipe. See make ahead instructions, below.

- 3 pounds sweet potatoes, peeled and cut into 1-inch cubes (about 9½ cups)
- 2½ pounds turnips, peeled and cut into 1-inch cubes (8½ cups)
- 3 tablespoons unsalted butter or regular butter
- 2 tablespoons unsalted butter or regular butter
- 2 tart, medium red cooking apples, cored and coarsely chopped
- ½ cup whole dates, pitted and snipped
- ¼ cup brown sugar
- 1 tablespoon lemon juice

Combine sweet potatoes, turnips, and enough water to cover in a 6- to 8-quart Dutch oven. Bring to boiling; reduce heat. Simmer, covered, for 12 to 15 minutes or until tender. Drain well in a very large colander. Return vegetables to the Dutch oven and add the 3 tablespoons butter and 1 teaspoon salt. Mash vegetables with a potato masher until nearly smooth.

For the relish, melt the 2 tablespoons butter in a medium skillet. Add apples, dates, and brown sugar. Cook and stir until sugar is dissolved and apples are just tender. Stir in lemon juice.

To serve, mound hot vegetables in a serving bowl and garnish center with the relish. Makes 10 to 12 servings.

TO MAKE AHEAD: Prepare vegetables as directed. Place in a 2- to 2½-quart microwave-safe dish; cool slightly, then cover and refrigerate. To reheat, microwave, covered, on 70% power (medium-high) for 20 to 25 minutes or until heated through, stirring twice. Make relish before serving.

Nutrition facts per serving: 238 cal., 6 g total fat (4 g sat. fat), 16 mg chol., 304 mg sodium, 46 g carbo., 9 g fiber, 3 g pro.

Spiced Pears and Camembert

✳

Take your pick—serve this as dessert, or serve it as a cheese course before dessert. Forelle and Seckel pears are two varieties that will work especially well. Choose 4-ounce pears and leave stems and cores intact so they'll hold their shape.

- 3 cups dry white wine
- 1 cup sugar
- ¼ cup coarsely chopped crystallized ginger
- 12 inches stick cinnamon, broken
- 8 whole allspice
- 8 whole cloves
- 8 cardamom pods, slightly crushed
- 8 small firm ripe pears, peeled Cranberries (optional)
- 1 8-ounce round Camembert cheese, cut into wedges

Combine the wine, sugar, ginger, cinnamon, allspice, cloves, and cardamom in a saucepan large enough to hold the pears. Cook, uncovered,* over medium heat to a gentle boil. Add the peeled pears. Return liquid just to boiling; reduce heat. Simmer, uncovered,* for 6 to 7 minutes or until pears are just fork-tender. Let the pears cool in the poaching liquid, turning, if necessary, to be sure all sides are moistened.

Transfer pears to a serving dish using a slotted spoon. Strain poaching liquid. Serve the pears slightly warm, at room temperature, or chilled, with the poaching liquid spooned over. If desired, surround the serving dish with cranberries. Accompany with cheese wedges. Makes 8 servings.

*Note: Be sure to cook the wine mixture uncovered to avoid the wine's vapors bursting into flames.

Nutrition facts per serving: 309 cal., 7 g total fat (4 g sat. fat), 20 mg chol., 245 mg sodium, 43 g carbo., 2 g fiber, 6 g pro.

73

Country Pumpkin Torte

✳

You can make the cake, icing, and Candied Orange Peel for this tall beauty ahead of time for later assembly.

2⅔ cups all-purpose flour
1 tablespoon baking powder
1 teaspoon pumpkin pie spice
¾ teaspoon baking soda
¾ teaspoon salt
¾ teaspoon ground cloves
1 cup shortening
1 cup packed brown sugar
¼ cup full-flavored molasses
4 eggs
1 cup milk
¾ cup canned pumpkin
1 tablespoon grated fresh ginger
1 recipe Cream Cheese Frosting (far right)
1 recipe Candied Orange Peel (page 129) (optional)

Preheat oven to 350°F. Grease and lightly flour three 9x1½-inch or 8x1½-inch round baking pans; set aside.

Combine flour, baking powder, pumpkin pie spice, baking soda, salt, and cloves in a medium mixing bowl; set aside.

Beat shortening in a large mixing bowl with an electric mixer on medium to high speed for 30 seconds. Add brown sugar and molasses; beat until smooth. Add eggs, 1 at a time, beating for 1 minute after each addition. Combine milk, pumpkin, and ginger in a small bowl. Add flour mixture and pumpkin mixture alternately to beaten mixture, beating on low speed after each addition until just combined. Pour batter evenly into prepared pans.

Bake for 22 to 28 minutes or until a wooden toothpick inserted near the center comes out clean. (If all 3 layers won't fit in oven at the same time, or if you don't have 3 pans, one-third of the batter may be covered and chilled for up to 45 minutes before baking.) Cool cakes in pans on wire racks for 10 minutes. Remove cakes from pans. Cool thoroughly on wire racks.

To assemble, place 1 cake layer on serving plate; spread with one-third of the Cream Cheese Frosting. Top with second layer cake; spread with one-third of the frosting. Top with third cake layer and remaining frosting. If desired, arrange Candied Orange Peel on top. Cover and store in the refrigerator. Makes 16 servings.

CREAM CHEESE FROSTING: Beat one 8-ounce package softened cream cheese, ½ cup softened butter, and 2 teaspoons vanilla in a large mixing bowl with an electric mixer on medium speed for 30 seconds. Slowly add 2 cups sifted powdered sugar and 1 tablespoon lemon juice, beating well. Add 2 cups additional sifted powdered sugar, beating well. If necessary, beat in additional powdered sugar or lemon juice until the frosting is easy to spread.

Nutrition facts per serving: 467 cal., 25 g total fat (11 g sat. fat), 85 mg chol., 356 mg sodium, 56 g carbo., 1 g fiber, 5 g pro.

Caramelized onions
and Brie

Artichoke hearts
and shredded
Parmigiano-
Reggiano

Roasted red pepper
and Italian parsley

Red and yellow
cherry tomatoes

Mozzarella with
pesto and basil

Tapenade and
green olives

Too busy to host a houseful? No problem! With this selection of appetizer recipes that range from off-the-shelf winners to make-ahead dazzlers, you'll have time to gather friends for some great fun during the holidays.

the eleventh hour *host*

Bites of Italy

✳

You can top the cheese crackers before baking as directed. Or bake the dough slices without toppings, and set out bowls of toppings instead. Then, invite your guests to top crackers after they're baked.

- ¼ cup butter (no substitutes), softened
- 4 ounces freshly grated Romano or Parmesan cheese
- 1 cup all-purpose flour
- 1½ teaspoons finely snipped fresh rosemary or sage
- ½ teaspoon finely shredded lemon peel
- ¼ teaspoon pepper
- 1 beaten egg
- ½ to ¾ cup topping, such as tapenade, sliced marinated artichoke hearts, basil or tomato pesto, sliced olives, fresh herbs, roasted garlic, caramelized onions, cherry tomatoes, herb sprigs, Brie, Parmigiano-Reggiano cheese, blanched asparagus tips, and/or roasted red pepper strips

Beat butter in a medium bowl with an electric mixer on medium speed for 30 seconds. Stir in Romano or Parmesan cheese, flour, rosemary or sage, lemon peel, and pepper until combined (mixture will be crumbly). Stir in egg. Form into a ball with your hands. Shape into a 9-inch-long log. Wrap tightly in plastic wrap and chill for 2 hours or until firm.

Preheat the oven to 425°F. Cut dough into ⅛-inch-thick slices with a sharp knife and place on an ungreased baking sheet. Top with ¼ to ½ teaspoon of desired topping. Bake in the preheated oven for 6 to 8 minutes or until golden. (Or bake dough slices without toppings, and top after baking.) Makes about 60.

TO MAKE AHEAD: Refrigerate unbaked dough wrapped tightly in plastic wrap up to 1 week or freeze up to 6 months. To serve, thaw in refrigerator before slicing and baking as directed above.

Nutrition facts per appetizer: 23 cal., 2 g total fat (1 g sat. fat), 7 mg chol., 43 mg sodium, 2 g carbo., 0 g fiber, 1 g pro.

from pantry to party

If you're crunched for time at the holidays, make one or two impressive appetizers (such as the Salmon-Dill Cheesecake, page 79) and round out the spread with purchased treats such as:

■ Jars of marinated eggplant slices, artichoke hearts, and/or roasted red peppers.

■ Boldly seasoned salamis or other dry cured meats that keep well.

■ Ready-made spreadables, such as jars of tapenade and baba ghanoush or tins of pâté.

■ Olives: You just can't go wrong with a mix of imported varieties.

■ Firm and hard cheeses: Properly wrapped and stored in the refrigerator, they generally keep longer than softer cheeses. Try aged Manchego, Gouda, and Asiago, or Parmigiano-Reggiano.

Quick-Fix
Focaccia Wedges

Quick-Fix Focaccia Wedges

✳

This one's ready in 20 minutes and made with ingredients that have long shelf lives.

- 3 medium onions, thinly sliced
- ¼ teaspoon coarsely ground pepper
- 1 tablespoon olive oil
- ¾ cup rinsed and drained canned white beans
- ½ cup dry white wine or reduced-sodium chicken broth
- 1 teaspoon dried thyme, crushed
- 4 6-inch Italian bread shells (such as Boboli brand)
  Red sweet pepper (optional)
  Fresh marjoram (optional)

Preheat oven to 450°F. Cook and stir onion and ground pepper in hot oil in a skillet over medium-high heat, uncovered, for 7 minutes or until onion turns brown. Remove onion; set aside. Add beans to skillet; cook 1 minute. Add wine or broth and thyme; reduce heat and simmer, uncovered, 3 to 4 minutes or until liquid is reduced by half. Mash beans slightly. Spread bread shells with bean mixture; top with onion. Bake in the preheated oven for 8 to 10 minutes. Cut into wedges. Garnish with red pepper and marjoram, if desired. Makes 16 servings.

Nutrition facts per serving: 102 cal., 3 g total fat (0 g sat. fat), 1 mg chol., 176 mg sodium, 15 g carbo., 1 g fiber, 4 g pro.

Wonton Dippers

✳

While you're at it, consider making a bonus batch. This recipe doubles easily and freezes well up to 2 months.

- 1 cup dried shiitake mushrooms
- ¼ pound fresh or frozen crabmeat, thawed and flaked, or ½ of an 8-ounce package flake-style imitation crabmeat
- 2 tablespoons finely chopped carrot
- 2 tablespoons chopped green onion
- 2 tablespoons finely chopped water chestnuts or celery
- 2 tablespoons snipped fresh cilantro
- 1 beaten egg white
- 1 tablespoon soy sauce
- 2 teaspoons grated fresh ginger
- 1 teaspoon toasted sesame oil
- ½ teaspoon Oriental chili paste
- ¼ teaspoon salt
- ¼ teaspoon pepper
- 32 wonton wrappers
  Cooking oil or shortening for frying
- 1 recipe Hoisin Dressing (right)

Soak mushrooms in a small bowl in enough warm water to cover for 30 minutes; drain and finely chop. For filling, combine mushrooms, crabmeat, carrot, green onion, water chestnuts or celery, cilantro, egg white, soy sauce, ginger, sesame oil, chili paste, salt, and pepper in a medium bowl.

Place 1 teaspoon of filling slightly off-center on a wonton wrapper. Fold wonton wrapper in half to enclose filling, and release any trapped air; moisten edges with water and press to seal. Place finished wontons in a single layer on a baking sheet lined with waxed paper. Cover lightly with plastic wrap while filling and sealing the remaining wonton wrappers.

Mandarin Beef Buns

Wonton Dippers

Heat 1½ to 2 inches of cooking oil or shortening in a 3-quart saucepan or wok over medium-high heat to 365°F. Fry wontons, a few at a time, in the hot oil about 1 minute or until crisp and golden, turning once. Drain on paper towels. Serve with dressing. Makes 32.

HOISIN DRESSING: Stir together ⅓ cup hoisin sauce, ¼ cup rice vinegar or red wine vinegar, 1 tablespoon soy sauce, 1 tablespoon prepared Chinese-style hot mustard or Dijon-style mustard, 1 tablespoon grated fresh ginger, 1 teaspoon sugar, ½ teaspoon pepper, and 2 cloves garlic, minced.

TO MAKE AHEAD: Prepare Wonton Dippers as directed through filling and sealing. Arrange unfried wontons in a single layer in an airtight container. Seal and freeze up to 2 months. Store Hoisin Dressing in an airtight container in the refrigerator up to 3 days, or freeze up to 2 months. To serve, thaw wontons overnight in the refrigerator, and fry as directed. Thaw Hoisin Dressing overnight in the refrigerator before using.

Nutrition facts per wonton: 72 cal., 4 g total fat (1 g sat. fat), 3 mg chol., 184 mg sodium, 7 g carbo., 0 g fiber, 2 g pro.

Mandarin Beef Buns

✳

These hearty bites are great for appetizer spreads that will stand in for dinner.

- 1 tablespoon cooking oil
- 2 cups shredded cooked beef or pork
- ¼ teaspoon crushed red pepper
- 1 cup chopped bok choy, Chinese cabbage, or green cabbage
- 2 tablespoons grated fresh ginger
- 1 teaspoon finely shredded orange peel
- ⅓ cup thinly bias-sliced green onions
- ¼ cup hoisin sauce
- 1 16-ounce package hot-roll mix
- 1 beaten egg
  Sesame seeds

For filling, heat oil in a large skillet over medium heat. Add beef or pork and red pepper; cook and stir for 3 minutes. Add bok choy or other cabbage, ginger, and orange peel. Cook and stir 2 to 3 minutes or until bok choy is wilted. Stir in green onions and hoisin sauce. Remove from heat; cool.

Meanwhile, prepare the hot-roll mix according to package directions. Divide dough into 24 portions. Shape each portion into a ball. On a lightly floured surface roll or pat each ball into a 3½-inch circle.

For each bun, place about 1 tablespoon filling in the center of a circle. Moisten edges of dough with water and bring up around filling, pinching edges together to seal.

Arrange filled buns, seam sides down, on 2 lightly greased baking sheets. Cover; let rise in a warm place for 20 minutes. Preheat oven to 375°F. Brush buns with beaten egg; sprinkle with sesame seeds. Bake 15 minutes or until golden. Serve warm. Makes 24 buns.

TO MAKE AHEAD: Prepare and bake Mandarin Beef Buns as directed. Remove from baking sheet; cool for 30 minutes on a wire rack. Wrap buns in heavy foil; freeze up to 1 month. To serve, leave the frozen buns in foil wrap. Bake in a 325° oven about 40 minutes or until buns are heated through.

Nutrition facts per bun: 126 cal., 4 g total fat (1 g sat. fat), 28 mg chol., 188 mg sodium, 16 g carbo., 0 g fiber, 7 g pro.

Italian-Style Marinated Shrimp and Artichokes

Baked Kasseri Cheese Spread

Baked Kasseri Cheese Spread

✳

Go ahead—pick up the phone and invite someone in to linger by the fire with a glass of red wine, a loaf of crusty bread, and this creamy melted-cheese spread.

- 12 ounces kasseri* or scamorze cheese
- ⅔ cup kalamata olives, pitted and quartered
- 2 tablespoons snipped fresh oregano
- 1 clove garlic, minced
- ¼ teaspoon crushed red pepper
  French bread, apples, or crackers

Preheat oven to 450°F. Cut cheese into ½-inch-thick slices. Layer cheese in the bottom of a shallow 1-quart quiche dish or a 9-inch pie plate, overlapping if necessary. Toss together the olives, oregano, garlic, and red pepper. Sprinkle over the cheese.

Bake in the preheated oven for 8 to 10 minutes or until cheese just begins to melt. Serve immediately on bread,

apples, or crackers; rewarm cheese as needed. Makes 12 servings.

*Note: Traditionally Greek, kasseri cheese is made with either sheep's or goat's milk. Its sharp, salty flavor and meltability make it a natural for this dish.

Nutrition facts per serving (spread only):
141 cal., 12 g total fat (7 g sat. fat), 30 mg chol., 350 mg sodium, 1 g carbo., 0 g fiber, 7 g pro.

Italian-Style Marinated Shrimp and Artichokes

✳

Long-keeping foods from the freezer, pantry, and fridge combine for these nibbles.

- 1 9-ounce package frozen artichoke hearts
- 1 8-ounce package frozen, peeled, deveined medium shrimp
- ½ of a 7- or 7½-ounce jar roasted red sweet peppers, drained and cut into thin strips (½ cup)
- ⅓ cup white wine vinegar or cider vinegar
- ¼ cup salad oil
- 1 clove garlic, minced, or ½ teaspoon bottled minced garlic

- 1 tablespoon thinly sliced green onion
- ½ teaspoon dried oregano or basil, crushed
- ¼ teaspoon salt
- ¼ teaspoon dry mustard (optional)
- ⅛ teaspoon pepper

Cook artichoke hearts in a large saucepan according to package directions. Add shrimp the last 3 to 4 minutes of cooking; cook until shrimp turn opaque and artichokes are tender. Drain well. When cool enough to handle, halve any large artichoke pieces. Combine artichokes, shrimp, and red pepper strips in a nonmetal bowl.

Combine vinegar, oil, garlic, onion, oregano or basil, salt, dry mustard (if desired), and pepper in a screw-top jar. Cover; shake to combine. Pour over artichoke mixture. Toss gently to coat. Cover; chill 2 to 4 hours; stir occasionally.

To serve, drain mixture and transfer to a shallow serving bowl or platter. Serve with a slotted spoon or picks, or, if desired, on leaves of Belgian endive. Makes 15 servings.

Nutrition facts per serving: 43 cal., 2 g total fat (0 g sat. fat), 23 mg chol., 53 mg sodium, 2 g carbo., 1 g fiber, 4 g pro.

Salmon-Dill Cheesecake

Salmon-Dill Cheesecake

✳

If you're looking for one impressive appetizer to star as the centerpiece of your spread, this is it. Make it up to 24 hours in advance; then round out the buffet with some of the simpler recipes on these pages and a few purchased goodies (see tip, page 75).

1½ cups finely crushed crispy rye or sesame crackers

6 tablespoons butter or margarine, melted

2 tablespoons grated Parmesan cheese

1 8-ounce package cream cheese, softened

2 eggs

½ of an 8-ounce tub cream cheese with salmon or plain tub cream cheese

1 tablespoon white wine vinegar or lemon juice

1 8-ounce carton dairy sour cream

4 ounces dry-smoked salmon, skin and bones removed and flaked

1 tablespoon snipped fresh dill
Dill sprigs (optional)
Salmon caviar (optional)

Preheat oven to 350°F.

For crust, combine crushed crackers, melted butter or margarine, and Parmesan cheese in a medium mixing bowl. Press mixture evenly on the bottom and about 1 inch up the side of a 9-inch springform pan. Set the pan aside.

For filling, beat softened cream cheese in a large mixing bowl with an electric mixer on low to medium speed until smooth. Add eggs all at once. Beat on low speed just until combined. Add tub cream cheese and vinegar or lemon juice, beating on low speed just until combined. Stir in sour cream, smoked salmon, and 1 tablespoon snipped dill.

Pour into crust-lined springform pan. Place the springform pan on a shallow baking pan on the oven rack. Bake in the preheated oven for 30 to 35 minutes or until center appears nearly set when gently shaken.

Remove springform pan from baking pan. Cool cheesecake on a wire rack for 15 minutes. Use a small metal spatula to loosen crust from side of pan. Cool 30 minutes more. Remove side of the springform pan. Cool 1 hour; cover and chill in the refrigerator for at least 2 hours. Garnish with fresh dill sprigs and salmon caviar, if desired. Makes 16 servings.

TO MAKE AHEAD: Prepare Salmon-Dill Cheesecake as directed, except cover and chill in the refrigerator for up to 24 hours. To serve, garnish cheesecake as directed.

Nutrition facts per serving: 202 cal., 16 g total fat (10 g sat. fat), 72 mg chol., 210 mg sodium, 9 g carbo., 2 g fiber, 5 g pro.

79

Foie Gras with Fig Toasts

a french *réveillon* dinner party

For a spectacular dinner party during the season, tap into a French tradition that will translate well to your holiday table.

Traditionally, the French fast before midnight mass on Christmas Eve; afterwards, they break the fast with their own brand of revelry, a festive dinner that lasts into the wee hours. This feast is aptly named the "Réveillon" (rev-ay-YON), or the wake up, and symbolically refers to the spiritual awakening to Christ's birth.

Traditions vary from region to region in France, but often appearing on the menu are festive foods such as oysters (a fresh, seasonal favorite this time of the year), foie gras (see tip, far right), and poultry with roasted chestnuts. All three star on our menu. For dessert, a cake in the shape of a log, known as the Bûche de Noël (or Yule Log), is a cherished tradition in Paris and nearby northern regions. In the South of France, families are more likely to top off their feast with a spread known as the "thirteen desserts," commemorating Christ and his 12 apostles. These vary from home to home and usually include fresh and dried fruits, nuts, pastries, and citrus-scented breads. We rolled many of these flavors into one terrific dessert, our Tuiles Towers with Spiced Fruit Compote, page 84.

Life in contemporary France makes it difficult to gather everyone on Christmas Eve, so many families save the feast until New Year's Eve. Our menu will make for a magical gathering no matter when you serve it during the holiday season.

Foie Gras with Fig Toasts

✳

Mixed greens, lightly dressed with vinaigrette, will complement the rich foie gras well. If you have a little foie gras leftover, sauté it and serve it with scrambled eggs for a decadent brunch-time treat.

    8 ½-inch-thick slices baguette-style
        French bread
   16 to 20 ounces fresh duck foie gras
        Sea salt and ground black
        pepper
    2 to 3 tablespoons fig preserves
        Sea salt and crushed pink
        peppercorns

Preheat oven to 350°F. Place bread slices on a cookie sheet. Bake in the preheated oven for 10 minutes or until crisp and lightly toasted. Cool.
Bias-slice 12 ounces of the foie gras crosswise into sixteen ½-inch-thick slices. (Cover and chill remaining foie gras for another use; use within 2 days.) Score each slice in a diamond pattern. Heat a heavy 10-inch nonstick skillet over medium-high heat until a drop of water in pan sizzles.
Place 6 of the slices in the hot skillet. Cook for 40 seconds; turn. Cook 40 seconds more. Remove from heat and transfer to serving platter; sprinkle lightly with salt and black pepper. Pour off fat from skillet. Repeat, cooking remaining foie gras slices. Serve immediately with toasted bread and preserves; pass additional sea salt and crushed peppercorns. Makes 8 servings.

Nutrition facts per serving: 246 cal., 19 g total fat (6 g sat. fat), 162 mg chol., 478 mg sodium, 12 g carbo., 0 g fiber, 6 g pro.

a french indulgence

■ Foie gras (pronounced "fwah-grah") literally means "fat liver." This traditional French treat is usually produced on small farms where the growers specially raise the ducks or geese by plumping them up with a rich, force-fed diet for 4 to 5 months. The process results in an oversize, fatty liver with silky, smooth, and rich qualities that make foie gras afficionados swoon.

Until recently, the only foie gras Americans could find was processed and canned. However, these days, American-produced fresh foie gras can be found in gourmet shops and on the Internet (see sources, page 158). Keep in mind that while fresh foie gras is easy to cook, it can shrink up quickly when overcooked, so watch carefully during cooking.

81

menu

Oysters with
Tomato-Fennel Relish

✳

Foie Gras with Fig Toasts

✳

Roasted Beet and Goat
Cheese Salad

✳

Braised Duck with
Vegetables and Chestnuts

✳

Gruyère-Garlic Mashed
Potatoes

✳

Tuiles Towers with Spiced
Fruit Compote

**To remove backbones of ducklings,
use** poultry shears or heavy kitchen
shears to cut on either side of the
backbone; discard bone. Quarter ducks
by cutting in half through breast bone;
then cut each half in half crosswise.
Remove and discard excess fat. With a
sharp knife score duck skin, cutting
through fat layer but not into meat. In a
large plastic bag combine flour, salt, and
pepper. Add duck, one piece at a time,
shaking to coat.

Heat oil in an 8- or 10-quart stew pot.
Add 3 or 4 of the duck pieces, fat side
down; brown on all sides. Remove
duck. Repeat with remaining duck
pieces. Drain off all but 1 tablespoon of
the fat.

Add garlic to pan and cook 30 seconds.
Carefully add chicken broth and wine
to pan, stirring to scrape up any
browned bits. Add bouquet garni.
Return duck pieces to pan. Bring to
boiling; reduce heat. Cover and simmer
over low heat 1¼ to 1½ hours or until
duck is just tender, rearranging pieces
halfway through cooking to assure
even cooking.

Oysters with Tomato-
Fennel Relish

✳

*The French often enjoy their oysters raw;
however, because raw oysters raise food
safety concerns, we decided to come up
with a French-inspired way to cook them.*

⅔ cup finely chopped, seeded
   fresh plum tomatoes
⅓ cup finely chopped fresh fennel
½ teaspoon finely shredded
   orange peel
1 tablespoon orange juice
2 teaspoons olive oil
1½ teaspoons snipped fresh chives
⅛ teaspoon salt
16 fresh oysters in shells
2 cloves garlic, minced
1 tablespoon butter

For relish, stir together the tomatoes,
fennel, orange peel, orange juice, olive
oil, chives, and salt in a small mixing
bowl. Cover and chill until needed, up
to 24 hours.

Thoroughly wash oysters. Using an
oyster knife or other blunt-tipped knife,
open shells. Remove oysters and dry.
Discard flat top shells; wash deep bottom
shells. (Oysters can be removed and
chilled up to 24 hours before cooking.)

Before serving, stir relish. Spoon
about 1 tablespoon relish in each bottom shell. Arrange on a platter.

Cook oysters and garlic in hot butter in
a large skillet for 2 to 3 minutes or until

edges of oysters curl and the surfaces of
the oysters begin to brown. Place a
cooked oyster atop relish in each shell.
Serve immediately. Makes 8 servings
(2 oysters each).

Nutrition facts per serving: 49 cal., 3 g total fat
(1 g sat. fat), 19 mg chol., 114 mg sodium,
3 g carbo., 1 g fiber, 2 g pro.

Braised Duck with
Vegetables and
Chestnuts

✳

*By roasting the duck in the oven
after braising it, the skin develops
an appetizing brown color and
crisper texture.*

2 4- to 5-pound ducklings
1 cup all-purpose flour
1 teaspoon salt
½ teaspoon pepper
2 tablespoons olive oil
3 cloves garlic, minced
3 cups chicken broth
1½ cups dry white wine
1 bouquet garni (see tip, right)
6 medium carrots, peeled and cut
   into julienne strips (3 cups)
3 6-ounce turnips, peeled and cut
   into julienne strips (3 cups)
1½ cups pearl onions, peeled*
16 whole peeled chestnuts, halved
   (1½ cups) (see tip, page 83)
   Snipped fresh thyme (optional)
1 recipe Gruyère-Garlic Mashed
   Potatoes (optional) (page 84)

bouquet garni

■ A bouquet garni (boo-KAY gar-
NEE) is a French term for a bundle
of herbs (traditionally, celery tops,
thyme, parsley, and bay leaf) that
are tied together in cheesecloth,
making it easy to remove the
herbs neatly from a cooked dish.
To make your own bouquet garni
for the braised duck recipe, cut a
square of 100-percent-cotton
cheesecloth. In the center place
two 2-inch celery sticks with
leaves, 4 sprigs fresh parsley,
2 sprigs fresh thyme, and 2 bay
leaves. Gather cheesecloth around
herbs and tie top with clean
kitchen string.

82

to boil chestnuts

■ If starting with fresh chestnuts in shells, use a sharp knife and carefully make a small slit in the flat side of each chestnut. In a medium saucepan combine chestnuts and enough water to cover. Bring to boiling; reduce heat. Boil gently for 8 minutes. Drain chestnuts; let cool. Carefully peel chestnuts.

Meanwhile, preheat oven to 450°F. Transfer duck to a roasting pan, reserving liquid in pot. Roast duck, uncovered, about 12 minutes or until browned and skin is slightly crisp. Meanwhile, add carrots, turnips, onions, and chestnuts to cooking liquid. Simmer, covered, 5 to 10 minutes or until vegetables are just tender. Remove vegetables with a slotted spoon; transfer to a serving bowl and keep warm. Discard bouquet garni. Strain cooking liquid through a wire mesh sieve; skim fat (you should have about 3 cups cooking liquid). Return sauce to pan. Boil, uncovered, about 5 minutes or until reduced to 2½ cups.

To serve, divide duck pieces and vegetables among shallow bowls or plates. Spoon sauce over top. Sprinkle each serving with some snipped fresh thyme, if desired. Serve with Gruyère-Garlic Mashed Potatoes, if desired. Makes 8 servings.

*Note: To peel pearl onions, place onions with peel in boiling water in a medium saucepan for 30 seconds. Drain and rinse with cold water. Cut off root end of the onions and squeeze from other end to remove peels.

Nutrition facts per serving: 582 cal., 23 g total fat (6 g sat. fat), 216 mg chol., 786 mg sodium, 37 g carbo., 5 g fiber, 47 g pro.

Roasted Beet and Goat Cheese Salad

✳

- 1 pound red baby beets or small beets, rinsed, trimmed, and peeled*
- 1 tablespoon olive oil
- ⅓ cup olive oil
- ¼ cup white wine vinegar
- 2 teaspoons Dijon-style mustard
- 2 tablespoons finely chopped shallots
- 10 cups baby salad greens (mesclun) or other mild salad greens
- 1 8-ounce tube semi-soft goat cheese (chèvre), cut into ¼-inch-thick rounds

Preheat oven to 425°F. If using small beets, halve or quarter. Place beets in a single layer in a shallow baking pan. Drizzle with the 1 tablespoon olive oil, tossing to coat. Season with salt and freshly ground pepper, tossing again. Cover with foil; roast 25 minutes. Uncover and roast 15 minutes or until fork-tender. Cool. Cut beets into bite-size strips. Place in a bowl; set aside.

For dressing, combine the ⅓ cup olive oil, the white wine vinegar, Dijon-style mustard, ¼ teaspoon salt, and ⅛ teaspoon freshly ground pepper in a screw-top jar. Cover and shake well.

Add shallots to beets; drizzle with 1 tablespoon of the dressing; toss to coat; set aside. Place greens in a very large bowl; drizzle with the remaining dressing. Toss to coat. Divide greens among 8 salad plates. Top each with cheese slices and beet mixture. Serves 8.

*Note: Baby beets do not need to be peeled.

Nutrition facts per serving: 237 cal., 19 g total fat (7 g sat. fat), 22 mg chol., 350 mg sodium, 8 g carbo., 2 g fiber, 8 g pro.

Roasted Beet and Goat Cheese Salad

83

Gruyère-Garlic
Mashed Potatoes

Braised Duck with
Vegetables and Chestnuts
(see recipe, page 82)

84

Tuiles Towers with
Spiced Fruit Compote

✳

*We took three beloved French foods:
pastry cream, tuiles (roof-tile shaped
cookies, pronounced TWEEL), and a
fruit compote reminiscent of the "thirteen
desserts" (see story, page 81), and made
one spectacular dessert!*

　3　egg whites
⅔　cup sugar
⅔　cup all-purpose flour
⅓　cup butter, melted
⅓　cup sliced almonds
　1　cup dry white wine
⅔　cup sugar
¼　cup water
　1　teaspoon finely shredded
　　　lemon peel
　1　2-inch stick cinnamon
　1　star anise
½　of a vanilla bean, split
　　　lengthwise
　2　small pears, cored and coarsely
　　　chopped
　6　dried light figs (calimyrna),
　　　stems removed and cut
　　　lengthwise into eighths
　2　dried plums (prunes), quartered
⅓　cup golden raisins
　1　recipe Vanilla Cream Filling
　　　(page 85)

Allow egg whites to stand at room
temperature for 30 minutes in a
medium mixing bowl.

Preheat oven to 375°F.

Line a cookie sheet with foil or
parchment paper. Lightly grease foil-
lined cookie sheet; set aside.

Beat egg whites with an electric mixer
on medium speed until soft peaks form
(tips curl). Gradually add the ⅔ cup
sugar, beating on high speed until stiff

Gruyère-Garlic
Mashed Potatoes

✳

*Gruyère—is it French or is it Swiss? Both
countries have vied for rights to the name
of this nutty-flavored cheese. But we
needn't fret about it—just enjoy it in
these downright decadent potatoes.*

3½　pounds potatoes, peeled and
　　　cut into 2-inch chunks (about
　　　10 medium potatoes)
¼　cup butter
　2　cloves garlic, minced
½　cup whole milk, half-and-half,
　　　or light cream
⅛　teaspoon pepper
1½　cups shredded Gruyère or Swiss
　　　cheese (6 ounces)

Cook potatoes, covered, in a small
amount of boiling lightly salted water
for 20 to 25 minutes or until tender.

Meanwhile, melt butter in a small
saucepan over medium heat. Add garlic
and cook for 2 minutes. Stir in milk,
¼ teaspoon salt, and the pepper. Cover
and keep warm on very low heat. (Do
not scorch.)

Drain potatoes; return to pan. Mash
with potato masher. Stir in warm garlic-
milk mixture. Fold in cheese. Cover and
let stand 5 minutes to allow the cheese
to melt. Serve with Braised Duck (see
recipe, page 82). Makes 8 servings.

Nutrition facts per serving: 269 cal., 14 g total fat
(8 g sat. fat), 42 mg chol., 221 mg sodium,
28 g carbo., 2 g fiber, 10 g pro.

peaks form (tips stand straight). Fold in about half of the flour. Gently stir in butter. Fold in remaining flour until thoroughly combined.

For each cookie, drop 1 tablespoon of batter onto the prepared cookie sheet. Using the back of a spoon, spread batter into 2½-inch circles. Sprinkle a few almonds atop each circle.

Bake about 7 minutes or until cookies are crisp and golden brown around edges. Let the cookies stand about 1 minute. Using a wide spatula, remove the cookies from baking sheet and place on a flat surface. (You will need to use a new sheet of parchment paper for each batch.) Cool completely. (Note: Although this recipe will make about 30 cookies, you will need only 24 for the dessert. Place extras in an airtight container and store up to 2 days.)

Combine wine, the ⅔ cup sugar, the water, lemon peel, stick cinnamon, star anise, and vanilla bean in a large non-reactive saucepan. Bring to boiling; reduce heat. Cover and simmer for 10 minutes. Using a fine mesh sieve, strain syrup. Return syrup to saucepan. Add fruits. Bring to boiling; reduce heat. Cover and simmer about 4 minutes or until pears are just tender. Remove from heat. Cool to room temperature. If desired, transfer to a glass jar or bowl. Cover and chill for up to 24 hours. Bring to room temperature before serving.

Prepare Vanilla Cream Filling as directed in recipe, above right.

Just before serving, place one cookie in the center of each of eight dessert plates. Spoon a scant ¼ cup of the Vanilla Cream Filling atop. Repeat layers; top with remaining cookies, using 3 cookies per serving. Spoon some of the fruit and syrup around the cookie tower on each plate. Spoon some of the syrup over each cookie tower.

VANILLA CREAM FILLING: Stir together ½ cup sugar, 2 tablespoons cornstarch, and ¼ teaspoon salt in a heavy small saucepan. Gradually stir in 2 cups half-and-half or light cream. Using a sharp knife, cut a lengthwise slit in ½ of a vanilla bean. Add vanilla bean to cream mixture.

Cook and stir over medium heat until thickened and bubbly. Cook and stir for 1 minute more. Gradually stir about half of the hot mixture into 4 beaten egg yolks. Return all of the yolk mixture to the saucepan. Bring to a gentle boil; reduce heat. Cook and stir for 2 minutes more. Remove from heat.

Remove and discard the vanilla bean. Transfer filling to a bowl. Cover surface with plastic wrap. Chill in the refrigerator for 2 to 3 hours or until cold (do not stir). Beat ⅓ cup whipping cream in a small mixing bowl with an electric mixer on medium speed until soft peaks form. Gradually add cooled filling, beating just until smooth; chill well before serving. Makes 8 servings.

Nutrition facts per serving: 574 cal., 24 g total fat (13 g sat. fat), 164 mg chol., 213 mg sodium, 80 g carbo., 4 g fiber, 8 g pro.

Tuiles Towers with Spiced Fruit Compote

85

This year, put the emphasis on entertaining rather than preparation. Reduce your stress level by using what you have or can easily buy in one brief trip; keep many of your table settings simple but creative; and most of all, have fun.

festive *tabletops*

Dinner parties invite guests to linger, relax, and share time and stories. Although a pretty table serves as the focal point of the evening, arranging one does not need to be an angst-filled operation. Start with the basics—your dinnerware. Pick a color, pattern, or theme from the plates you will use and make that the inspiration for the rest of the table. Freely mix and match a bit to keep the table from looking showroom perfect and altogether impersonal.

The delicate pattern and colors of the floral china shown here dictate that the table's other items be subtle enough to complement without overpowering the dinnerware. Matte-finish ornaments are the perfect solution. A curlicue wire tree brings color all the way to the top without blocking conversation or appearing too massive for the other embellishments. Anchored on both sides by clear bowls filled with additional balls, the tree and candle centerpiece couldn't be easier to assemble. Scattering more ornaments on beds of greens, or simply along the table, allows the color to flow from end to end.

impromptu compote

~ Turn your serving pieces upside down when searching for centerpiece ideas. This "compote" is a shallow bowl perched on a tall slender bowl. The pedestal bowl sits on its rim to stabilize the arrangement. Even though the compote doesn't match the round bowl, *opposite*, the shared knobby pattern ties them together. When stacking serving pieces, bowls, and plates, secure them with a dot of wax, the kind that's used to keep candles upright in candleholders.

global warming

❧ Round votive cups mimic the globe shapes while adding twinkle to the table. Tint water with blue food coloring and stir it to distribute the color. Fill each cup with blue-tinted water and place a small floating candle in the cup. Keep the flames low and well away from any flammable items. Never leave lit candles unattended.

greetings!

❧ Wish each guest a Happy New Year in a different language. Hand-letter an assortment of greetings or print them on the computer. Cut the phrases into long, narrow strips and tuck them under napkin rings. Here are a few common greetings; look for others in foreign language dictionaries and on Internet websites.

Dutch: *Gelukkig Niew Jaar*
German: *Frohliche Wunsche Zum Jahreswechsel*
Spanish: *Feliz Año Nuevo*
Italian: *Buon Capo-d'Anno*
French: *Souhaits de Bonne Annee*

89

worldly new year

Make a toast to peace and worldwide unity with a table that celebrates the arrival of a new year around the globe. Set clocks to different time zones so you'll know when midnight strikes in several locales. World-theme wallpaper and a wallpaper border form the tablecloth and runner here; maps or a plain cloth stamped with global designs would work equally well. Add globes and items that resemble them, such as foil globe-wrapped candies and round votives.

berry bright

For a perky trim that takes only minutes, ring white candles with cranberries and gold wire. Cut two strands of 8 mm gold wire for each candle, making the strands several inches longer than the candle circumference. String fresh cranberries onto the wires. Wrap the wires around the candles without crushing the berries. Twist the wire ends together to hold the rings against the candles.

chair bow

The back of the dining chair is visible, so decorate it with a small garland. For each swag, cut two pieces of soft long-needled evergreen, each about 12 inches long. Overlap the stems to form an arched swag and wire the greens together with floral wire. Tie the greens to the chair back with wide sheer ribbon. For upholstered chairs, carefully pin the ribbon to the chair. Tuck clusters of white allium into the bow and greenery.

napkin wrap

Give a new twist to the concept of napkin rings. For each napkin ring, cut 13 inches of medium-gauge floral wire. Place two jingle bells on one end of the wire and loop the wire back for the end of the ring. Wind the wire around a broom handle to curl it, then unwrap it to the desired shape. String cranberries onto the wire. End with two more jingle bells. Refrigerate the napkin rings until ready to use to prevent juices from bleeding.

90

spiral tree

A whimsical little tree brings a giggle to each place setting. Cut 4½ yards of 8 mm wire, double it, and twist the two strands together. Bend the wire at a right angle 20 inches from one end and shape the base. Measure up 7 inches from the base and bend the wire down to form the tip of the tree. Spiral the remaining wire around the "trunk." Slide cranberries onto the tree and adjust it for balance.

packaged berries

Use fresh cranberries for oversize holly berries on an elegantly wrapped package. Tie wide ribbon around the package, ending in a knot at the top. Arrange holly leaves around the knot and hot-glue them in place. Glue small pinecones and cranberries over the leaves and knot. Trim the ends of the ribbon.

holly berries

Decorate the end of a buffet table with a garland of holly leaves and cranberries. Using a double strand of carpet thread and a tapestry needle, randomly string cranberries and holly leaves onto the thread. Refrigerate the garland until just before guests arrive to prevent juice from bleeding. To attach the garland to the tablecloth, work from the underside. Hold the garland in place and pin it to the cloth with safety pins, hiding pins beneath the holly leaves.

star attraction

❧   Red and gold are tops when it comes to setting a holiday table. Adding unexpected elements makes the colors even more stunning. Sandwich flat cedar sprigs between gold chargers and transparent glass plates that have textured edges. Top each plate with a wire star that guests can take home at the end of the evening. For each star, cut 50 inches of 8 mm gold wire. Bend the wire in half and twist the strands together. Shape the wire into a star with each point of the star measuring about three inches. Twist the beginning and ending wires together to form a hanging loop. Carefully push a fresh cranberry onto each point, pinching the point if needed. Thread a 10-inch hanging ribbon through the loop.

ruby reds

❧ Once upon a time, pink and red never kept company on the same table. Now, thanks to a more relaxed and artistic attitude, almost anything goes. Antique ruby stemware was the starting point for this table. Reproduction salad plates in the same color give the stemware even more presence. The gold beaded rim of the plate at the next level echoes the ball-shape edging of the ruby stemware. Other hints of gold on the flatware, the mirrors reflecting the centerpiece and menu cards, and the star ornament nestled on the plate add to the richness. Shades of pink mixed in give the layers of color depth that red alone could never carry off.

◀ Tabletop Tree. Sprigs of nearly any greenery can be used to make a tiny tree. Select and dampen a floral foam cone to fit your container and glue it to the bottom. Wedge scraps of floral foam into the pot. Clip small branches of greenery and insert them into the foam. Trim the leaves or needles to maintain a conical shape, then add ornaments.

In a Twinkling

around the house

▲ All-Around Decorating. An antique sifter frames wintery items for a cold-weather display. (A shallow basket works as well.) Wire mixed greens to the woven portion to form a bed. Tie on mittens or other outdoor items for a long-lasting arrangement.

◀ Collector's Dream. Treasured collectibles don't need to be hidden during the holidays. Instead, use them as inspiration for Christmas decorating. Here a flow-blue platter and antique candlesticks keep their favored spots. A garland across the mantel, bows on the candlesticks, and stockings made from worn quilts augment the display and give it a festive look that blends with the rest of the room.

▲ Colonial Roots. Vary a traditional colonial centerpiece by sugar-frosting the fruits. Brush fresh fruit with beaten egg white, then roll it in superfine sugar until it looks as if it were dusted with snow. Let the fruit dry on a rack. Nestle the fruits in a bowl of greens, with a few spilling out onto the table.

▲ Stocking Valance. Tiny stockings hung from twine take the place of a café curtain or valance. Sew the stockings from vintage fabrics, clothing, and draperies. There's no need to line them since they're purely decorative.

▲ Pretty Patchwork. Gather your fabric scraps and piece them into blocks or strips of patchwork. For the star pillow, cut two shapes from patchwork. Sew piping to the front, sew the front to the back, and fill it with fiberfill or a pillow form. Tuft the center with a large button. To coordinate, sew patchwork strips to a purchased throw. Embroider "Let Christmas be a patchwork of memories" across one end.

▲ Fragrant Fruits. Pomanders and dried fruits look as great as they smell. For pomanders, pierce fresh citrus fruit with a skewer and press whole cloves into the holes. Sprinkle the pomanders with an equal mixture of cinnamon and allspice for more fragrance and to seal in the juice.

▶ Festive Topiary. Teeny topiaries sprout up at florists, nurseries, and even grocery stores during this time of year. Personalize yours with elements you would use on a full-size tree, only smaller. Little glass balls and bows deck out the tree here. Miniature garlands, undersize ornaments, and even dollhouse miniatures work just as well.

a taste of
two cultures
for hanukkah

Moroccan Lamb Roast

Latke "Macaroons"
(see recipe, page 98)

Jewish culture shares Middle Eastern and Eastern European influences. This Hanukkah feast brings distinctive foods and flavors from both regions to the table for one wonderful meal.

Moroccan Lamb Roast

✳

The centerpiece of this menu is a succulent roast of lamb rubbed with Moroccan-style spices.

- 1 5-pound bone-in leg of lamb
- 4 to 8 cloves garlic, peeled and cut into slivers
- 2 tablespoons coriander seeds, crushed
- 2 tablespoons finely shredded lemon peel
- 1 tablespoon olive oil
- 1 teaspoon cumin seeds, crushed
- ½ teaspoon salt
- ½ teaspoon whole black peppercorns, crushed
  Assorted peeled and cut-up vegetables, such as carrots, turnips, and sweet peppers (optional)

Trim excess fat from lamb. Cut several ½-inch-wide slits randomly into top and sides of roast. Insert garlic slivers into slits. Stir together coriander seeds, lemon peel, olive oil, cumin seeds, salt, and pepper in a small bowl. Rub lamb surface with spice mixture. Cover and chill for several hours or overnight, if desired.

Preheat oven to 350°F. Place lamb on a rack in a shallow roasting pan. Roast lamb in the preheated oven for 1¾ to 2¼ hours or until a meat thermometer inserted in the thickest portion of the meat registers 140°F for medium-rare doneness or 155°F for medium doneness. If desired, add assorted cut-up vegetables during last 45 minutes of cooking.

Remove lamb from oven. Loosely cover with foil. Let stand for 10 minutes (the temperature of the meat will rise about 5°F during standing time). Slice and serve lamb with the roasted vegetables, if desired. Serves 10.

Nutrition facts per serving: 235 cal., 10 g total fat (3 g sat. fat), 101 mg chol., 185 mg sodium, 1 g carbo., 0 g fiber, 32 g pro.

menu

Mediterranean Walnut Spread with Moroccan Pita Chips

✳

Beet Borscht

✳

Moroccan Lamb Roast with Mixed Roasted Vegetables

✳

Latke "Macaroons"

✳

Sweet Cheese Blintzes

2 tablespoons of the potato mixture into 1½-inch "haystacks," squeezing out slightly more than half of liquid as you shape (see photo 2, below). Place latkes on a greased, shallow baking pan.

Bake in the preheated oven for 45 minutes or until golden brown. Serve with lamb and roasted vegetables, if desired. Makes 12 macaroons.

*Note: Use russet or long white potatoes. They're lower in moisture than other varieties. Using higher-moisture potatoes may make the macaroons gummy.

Nutrition facts per macaroon: 61 cal., 1 g total fat (0 g sat. fat), 13 mg chol., 107 mg sodium, 11 g carbo., 1 g fiber, 1 g pro.

![Beet Borscht photo]

Beet Borscht

Latke "Macaroons"
✳

Hailing from Eastern Europe, latkes—fried potato pancakes—are a tasty Hanukkah tradition. Here, they get a clever makeover to resemble macaroons, the Jewish Passover treat.

    4 large potatoes* (about
         2 pounds)
    1 egg
    1 tablespoon olive oil
    ¾ teaspoon salt

Preheat oven to 350°F. Peel potatoes. Shred lengthwise into fine, long strands (see photo 1, above right). Place shredded potatoes in a colander. Rinse well with cold water. Press to remove as much liquid as possible.

Beat egg in a medium mixing bowl with olive oil and salt. Add the shredded potatoes to egg mixture. Using your hands, gently form 1 to

here's how...

Starting with the tip of the potato, shred the whole length of the potato along grater's surface. Use a smooth motion that follows the potato's natural curve. Turn potato often for easier gripping.

Measure the potato mixture and place in your hand. Squeeze out slightly more than half the liquid. Gently fluff the potato mixture, then shape loosely into a "haystack" about 1½ inches high.

Beet Borscht
✳

Depending on the sugar content of the beets used, you may want to adjust the amount of sugar to taste.

    3 pounds beets, trimmed
         and peeled
    3 medium onions, halved
         lengthwise (about 1 pound)
    1 teaspoon salt
    10 cups water
    ¼ cup sugar
    ¼ cup lemon juice
    1½ cups finely shredded green
         cabbage

Combine beets, onions, and salt in a 6- to 8-quart Dutch oven. Add water. Bring to boiling; reduce heat to medium-low. Cover and simmer for 20 minutes. Remove beets; carefully cut into large pieces; return to liquid. Stir in sugar and lemon juice. Return to boiling; reduce heat. Simmer, uncovered, for 10 minutes. Cover and chill, if desired.

To serve, ladle soup into bowls; use 1 onion half per serving. Sprinkle with cabbage. Makes 8 side-dish servings.

Nutrition facts per serving: 97 cal., 0 g total fat (0 g sat. fat), 0 mg chol., 388 mg sodium, 23 g carbo., 4 g fiber, 3 g pro.

Mediterranean Walnut Spread
✳

    1 cup canned garbanzo beans
         (about ½ of a 15-ounce can)
    ½ cup chopped walnuts
    ½ cup lightly packed basil leaves
    2 tablespoons olive oil
    2 to 3 teaspoons lemon juice
    ⅛ teaspoon salt
    ⅛ teaspoon pepper
       Toasted thin baguette slices, pita
         bread slices, or Moroccan Pita
         Chips (page 99)

Drain garbanzo beans, reserving the liquid. Combine beans and

2 tablespoons of the reserved liquid, the walnuts, basil leaves, olive oil, lemon juice, salt, and pepper in a blender container or food processor bowl. Cover and thoroughly blend or process. (Scrape down sides and add additional reserved liquid if mixture appears stiff.)

Serve spread on desired bread. Or place in an airtight container and store in the refrigerator up to 5 days. Makes 1¼ cups (20 servings).

Note: The spread can be made several days in advance. Let it come to room temperature before serving.

Nutrition facts per serving: 34 cal., 3 g total fat (0 g sat. fat), 0 mg chol., 25 mg sodium, 1 g carbo., 1 g fiber, 1 g pro.

Mediterranean Walnut Spread with Moroccan Pita Chips

Moroccan Pita Chips

✵

Throughout the holidays, keep these ingredients on hand and use them to quickly and easily convert simple pita bread rounds into well-seasoned chips.

¼ cup olive oil
½ teaspoon curry powder
¼ teaspoon ground cumin
¼ teaspoon ground red pepper
3 whole wheat or regular pita bread rounds

Preheat oven to 350°F.

Stir together olive oil, curry powder, cumin, and ground red pepper. Split pita bread rounds in half horizontally. Brush both sides of each cut round with oil mixture. Stack rounds; cut stack into eight wedges. Arrange half of the wedges in a single layer on a 15x10x1-inch baking pan. Bake in the preheated oven 8 to 10 minutes or until crisp. Repeat with remaining wedges. Store in an airtight container up to 1 week. Makes 48 (8 servings).

Nutrition facts per serving (6 chips): 124 cal., 8 g total fat (1 g sat. fat), 0 mg chol., 128 mg sodium, 13 g carbo., 2 g fiber, 2 g pro.

Sweet Cheese Blintzes

✵

According to Jewish dietary law, recipes with dairy products may not be eaten with or following meals featuring meat.

1 8-ounce carton mascarpone or cottage cheese
1 tablespoon honey
1 tablespoon milk
½ teaspoon finely shredded lemon peel
¼ teaspoon anise seeds, crushed
¾ cup all-purpose flour
½ teaspoon baking powder
1 egg white
¾ cup milk
1 egg yolk
2 teaspoons walnut oil or hazelnut oil
1½ teaspoons granulated sugar
½ teaspoon vanilla
Nonstick cooking spray
1 cup green grapes, sliced
Powdered sugar

For filling, beat together cheese, honey, the 1 tablespoon milk, lemon peel, and anise seeds. Cover; set aside.

For blintzes, stir together flour and baking powder; set aside. Beat egg white with an electric mixer on medium to high speed until soft peaks form.

Combine the ¾ cup milk, egg yolk, oil, granulated sugar, and vanilla. Beat with electric mixer until well combined. Add flour mixture; beat just until smooth. Fold in beaten egg white (texture should be that of a milk shake).

Spray a nonstick griddle or skillet with nonstick spray. Heat over medium heat 1 to 2 minutes. For each blintz, pour about 2 tablespoons batter onto griddle. Quickly spread batter to 4- to 5-inch circle. Cook about 30 seconds or until light brown. Gently turn with a spatula; cook 15 seconds. Invert blintz onto a plate lined with paper towels. Repeat with remaining batter to make 10 to 12 blintzes. (You may cook up to 3 or 4 blintzes at a time in a large skillet.) Place a dry paper towel between blintzes. Cover; keep warm.

Spoon 1 slightly rounded tablespoon of the filling across pancake just below center. Fold bottom of pancake over filling. Fold in sides; roll up. Arrange blintzes, seam-side down, on dessert plates. Top with grapes. Sprinkle with powdered sugar. Serve warm or at room temperature. Makes 10 to 12.

Nutrition facts per serving: 150 cal., 10 g total fat (5 g sat. fat), 43 mg chol., 40 mg sodium, 12 g carbo., 0 g fiber, 6 g pro.

99

Florentines

Austria's Linzer Torte is rolled into one great cookie; Italy's Florentines get a bonus swirl of white chocolate. And wait until you see what we've done to the Madeleine! Here, beloved European traditions are dressed up with new touches for the holidays.

old world cookies *with a new* twist

Florentines

✳

For a twist on tradition, our version adds a swirl of white chocolate to the dark chocolate that usually coats these chewy gems.

⅓ cup butter
⅓ cup milk
¼ cup sugar
2 tablespoons honey
¾ cup sliced almonds
½ cup finely chopped candied
    mixed fruits and peels
¼ cup all-purpose flour
¾ cup semisweet chocolate pieces
2 tablespoons shortening
2 ounces white baking squares
2 teaspoons shortening

Preheat oven to 350°F.

Grease and lightly flour a cookie sheet or line with parchment paper; set aside. Combine butter, milk, sugar, and honey in a medium saucepan. Bring to a full rolling boil, stirring occasionally. Remove from heat. Stir in almonds and candied fruits and peels. Stir in flour.

Drop batter by level tablespoons at least 3 inches apart onto prepared sheet. Using the back of a spoon or a thin metal spatula, spread the batter into 3-inch circles.

Bake in the preheated oven for 7 to 9 minutes or until the edges are lightly browned. Cool on cookie sheet 2 minutes. Carefully transfer to waxed paper or remove parchment with cookies. Cool thoroughly.

Repeat with the remaining batter, greasing and flouring or re-lining the cookie sheet between batches.

Heat semisweet chocolate pieces and the 2 tablespoons shortening in a small heavy saucepan over low heat until melted, stirring occasionally. Turn cookies, bottom sides up. Spread the bottom of each cookie with about 1 teaspoon of the chocolate mixture. Or dip cookie halfway into the chocolate mixture.

Melt white baking squares and the 2 teaspoons shortening in another small saucepan; drizzle onto dark chocolate. To marble, draw the tines of a fork across the white drizzle. (Do not marble the dipped cookies; just drizzle the dipped part with the white chocolate.) Store, covered, in the refrigerator. Makes 20 cookies.

Viola Shortbread

The beloved teatime cookie from Britain is made even more lovely with edible flowers, which you can find year-round in many produce aisles. Find dried egg whites in the baking aisle.

1¼ cups all-purpose flour
3 tablespoons granulated sugar
½ cup butter (no substitutes)
1 tablespoon dried egg whites
2 tablespoons water
12 or 16 edible violas or other edible flowers
Fine sanding sugar

Preheat oven to 325°F.
Combine flour and granulated sugar in a medium mixing bowl. Using a pastry cutter, cut in butter until the mixture resembles fine crumbs and starts to cling together. Form the mixture into a ball and knead until smooth.

Pat or roll dough into an 8-inch circle on an ungreased cookie sheet. Using your fingers, press to make a scalloped edge. Cut circle into 12 or 16 wedges; do not separate.
Bake in the preheated oven for 25 to 30 minutes or until bottom just starts to brown and center is set. Cut circle into wedges again while warm. Cool on cookie sheet on a wire rack.
Combine dried egg whites and water in a small bowl. Brush tops of wedges with egg white mixture. Place violas on top; brush with more egg mixture. Sprinkle with fine sanding sugar. Bake in the 325°F oven for 5 minutes. Transfer to wire racks; cool. Makes 12 or 16 cookies.

Viola Shortbread.

Linzer Bars

This is a bar-cookie take on Austrian Linzer Torte. For photo and a clever presentation idea, see page 131.

⅔ cup butter (no substitutes)
⅔ cup granulated sugar
½ teaspoon ground cinnamon
¼ teaspoon ground cloves
1 egg
1 tablespoon cherry liqueur, cherry brandy, or water
1½ cups all-purpose flour
1 cup ground hazelnuts (filberts) or almonds
1 teaspoon finely shredded lemon peel
2 tablespoons all-purpose flour
1 cup seedless red raspberry jam
Powdered sugar (optional)

Beat butter with an electric mixer on medium to high speed 30 seconds. Add granulated sugar, cinnamon, and cloves; beat until combined. Beat in egg and liqueur until combined. Stir in 1½ cups flour, hazelnuts and peel with wooden spoon. Divide dough in half; stir the 2 tablespoons flour into one portion of the dough. Wrap doughs in plastic wrap (label the one with additional flour); chill for 1 hour.
Roll the dough with the added flour between 2 pieces of waxed paper into a 15x10-inch rectangle. Remove top piece of waxed paper. Cut rectangle into 10x½-inch strips. Slide dough, with waxed paper, onto a large baking sheet. Chill strips about 15 minutes or until firm and easy to handle.
Meanwhile, preheat oven to 350°F. Line a 13x9x2-inch baking pan with foil, extending foil 1 inch beyond ends of pan. Grease foil. Pat the dough without the added 2 tablespoons flour into the bottom of the greased foil-lined pan. Spread jam evenly over dough in pan.
Peel dough strips from waxed paper using a long narrow-bladed metal spatula. Carefully place half of strips

Austrian Cookie Tarts

across jam about ½ inches apart. Trim ends and piece strips of dough together as necessary by overlapping slightly. Place remaining strips diagonally across pan, forming diamonds.

Bake in the preheated oven about 30 minutes or until crust is golden. Cool in pan on a wire rack. Lift out bars using foil. Cut into bars. Carefully remove foil. Just before serving, sift with powdered sugar, if desired. Makes 32.

Austrian Cookie Tarts
✳

These two-tone delights get more delicious with a few days' aging.

    1 recipe Browned Butter Spice
       Dough (below)
    1 recipe Plain Butter Dough
       (right)
    ½ cup raspberry or apricot
       preserves
       Sifted powdered sugar

Preheat oven to 375°F. Roll each portion of dough on a lightly floured surface to ⅛-inch thickness. Using 2½- to 3-inch cookie cutters with scalloped edges, cut dough into shapes. (Make matching cutout shapes from each dough.) Using ½-inch aspic cutters, cut 3 shapes from center of each Plain Butter Dough cutout (do not make cutouts in Browned Butter Spice Dough). Place 1 inch apart on an ungreased cookie sheet.

Bake in the preheated oven 7 to 8 minutes or until edges are very lightly browned. Transfer cookies to a wire rack; cool. Spread about 1 teaspoon preserves on bottom of each spice cookie. Top each with a plain cookie, bottom side down. Just before serving, generously sift powdered sugar atop. Makes about 20 sandwich cookies.

BROWNED BUTTER SPICE DOUGH: Heat ½ cup butter in a small saucepan over medium heat until butter turns color of light brown sugar. Remove from heat. Pour into a bowl; chill until butter resolidifies. Beat browned butter on medium to high speed 30 seconds. Add ½ cup sifted powdered sugar, 1 egg yolk, 1 teaspoon vanilla, ¼ teaspoon ground cinnamon, ⅛ teaspoon salt, and ⅛ teaspoon ground cloves. Beat until fluffy. Beat in as much of ¾ cup all-purpose flour as you can with a mixer. Stir in any remaining flour. Wrap dough in plastic wrap or waxed paper; chill 1 hour or until dough is easy to handle.

PLAIN BUTTER DOUGH: Beat ½ cup softened butter with an electric mixer on medium to high speed 30 seconds. Add ½ cup sifted powdered sugar, 1 egg yolk, 1 teaspoon vanilla, and ⅛ teaspoon salt. Beat until fluffy. Beat in as much of 1¼ cups all-purpose flour as you can with a mixer. Stir in any remaining flour. Wrap dough in plastic wrap or waxed paper; chill about 1 hour or until dough is easy to handle.

Cherry-Nut Rugelach
✳

Rugelach are often made with raisins, but dried apricots and cherries add an extra-festive note to this Hanukkah cookie.

    1 cup dried cherries and/or dried
       apricots, finely snipped
    ¼ cup sugar
    ¼ cup water
    2 teaspoons kirsch (optional)
    ½ cup finely chopped walnuts
    1 cup butter (no substitutes),
       softened
    1 3-ounce package cream
       cheese, softened
    2 cups all-purpose flour
    2 tablespoons sugar
       Milk
       Sugar (optional)

Preheat oven to 350°F. For filling, combine dried cherries and/or apricots, the ¼ cup sugar, and the water in a small saucepan. Bring to boiling.

Reduce heat; simmer, uncovered, for 5 minutes or until thickened, stirring occasionally. Remove from heat and stir in kirsch, if desired; cool. Stir in nuts.

For pastry, beat butter and cream cheese in a medium mixing bowl with an electric mixer on medium speed until combined. Add flour and the 2 tablespoons sugar; beat on low speed until crumbly, then knead until a dough forms. Divide dough into thirds.

Roll one-third of the dough on a lightly floured surface into a 9-inch circle. Spread dough with one-third of cooled filling. Cut circle into 12 wedge-shape pieces. Beginning at wide end of each wedge, roll up dough. Place cookies, tip side down, about 2 inches apart on a greased cookie sheet. Repeat with remaining dough and filling. Brush each cookie with some milk and, if desired, sprinkle with sugar.

Bake in the preheated oven for 15 minutes or until golden brown. Transfer to wire racks; cool. Makes 36.

103

Cherry-Nut Rugelach

Santa Madeleines

Santa Madeleines

✳

Ho, ho, ho! Who can resist these jolly, cherry-cheeked Santas, especially since they're made from a beloved cakelike little cookie from France?

- ¾ cup all-purpose flour
- ¼ teaspoon baking powder
- 1 egg
- 2 egg yolks
- 1 cup sifted powdered sugar
- ½ cup butter, melted and cooled
- 2 teaspoons finely shredded orange peel
- 2 teaspoons orange juice
- ½ teaspoon anise seeds, crushed (optional)
- 1 recipe Decorator Frosting (below right) or 2 cans vanilla frosting
  Red, blue, green, and/or black paste food coloring
  Small round candies (optional)

Preheat oven to 375°F. Grease and flour twenty-four 3-inch madeleine molds; set aside. Stir together flour and baking powder; set aside.

Beat egg and egg yolks in a medium mixing bowl with an electric mixer on high speed 5 minutes or until thick and lemon colored. Add powdered sugar; beat on low speed until combined, then on high speed about 5 minutes more or

until very thick and satiny. Beat in butter with an electric mixer on low speed. Add flour mixture, beating at low speed until combined. Stir in orange peel, orange juice, and, if using, anise seeds. Carefully spoon batter into the prepared molds, filling each three-fourths full. **Bake** in the preheated oven about 10 minutes or until edges are golden and tops spring back. Cool in molds on rack 1 minute. Loosen cookies with a knife. Invert cookies onto a rack and cool completely.

Divide frosting, leaving about half of it white; color one-third with red food coloring and remaining with green, black, and/or blue food coloring.

To decorate, fill a decorating bag fitted with a small star tip with white frosting. Pipe on hat trim at an angle about one third of the way down from narrow end of cookie. Fill decorating bag fitted with a small star tip or plain tip with red or pink frosting; pipe on hat. With white frosting, pipe on mustache, beard, and pom-pom.

Fill decorating bag fitted with a small round tip with green, black, or blue frosting; pipe on eyes. Using red frosting, pipe on mouth. Pipe on other frosting decorations. (Or use small round candies for eyes, nose, mouth, and cheeks, attaching them with frosting.) Wrap cookies tightly to store. Makes 24 cookies.

DECORATOR FROSTING: Beat 1 cup shortening and 1½ teaspoons vanilla on medium speed for 30 seconds. Slowly add 2 cups sifted powdered sugar; beat well. Beat in 2 tablespoons milk. Gradually beat in 2½ cups sifted powdered sugar and enough milk to make piping consistency.

Christmas Biscotti

✳

Italy's twice-baked treats get extra holiday cheer with cranberries and pistachio nuts.

- ⅓ cup butter
- ⅔ cup Vanilla Sugar (recipe, right)
- 2 teaspoons baking powder
- ½ teaspoon ground cardamom
- 2 eggs
- 2 cups all-purpose flour
- ¾ cup dried cranberries or snipped dried cherries
- ¾ cup chopped pistachio nuts

Preheat oven to 375°F. Beat butter with an electric mixer on medium speed for 30 seconds. Add the ⅔ cup Vanilla Sugar, the baking powder, and cardamom; beat until combined. Beat in eggs. Beat in as much of the flour as you can with the mixer. Stir in any remaining flour and the cranberries and nuts until combined. Divide dough in half. If necessary, cover and chill dough until easy to handle.

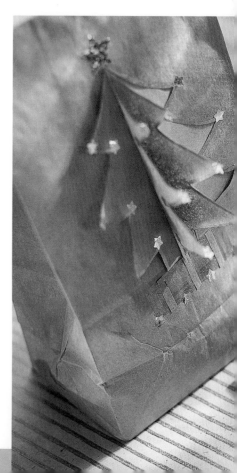

104

Shape each portion of dough into a 9-inch roll. Place 4 inches apart on a lightly greased cookie sheet, flattening slightly until 2 inches wide.

Bake in the preheated oven 25 to 30 minutes or until a wooden toothpick inserted near center comes out clean. Cool loaves on cookie sheet for 1 hour.

Preheat oven to 325°F. Cut each loaf diagonally into ½-inch slices using a serrated knife. Place slices, cut sides down, on an ungreased cookie sheet. Bake in the preheated oven 8 minutes. Turn slices over; bake 8 to 10 minutes more or until dry and crisp. Transfer to wire racks; cool. Store in a tightly covered container at room temperature up to 3 days or in the freezer up to 3 months. Makes about 32.

VANILLA SUGAR: Fill a quart jar with 4 cups sugar. Cut a vanilla bean in half lengthwise; insert into sugar. Secure lid. Store in a cool dry place for several weeks before using. Keeps indefinitely.

Christmas Biscotti

the flavors and colors of
kwanza

A relatively new holiday that was conceived in 1966, Kwanza honors African-American history and culture while celebrating the ties between family and friends. Although Kwanza traditions are still evolving, generally, the celebration includes songs, dances, stories, and crafted gifts reflecting African-American heritage. Food is also key to the celebration, and the flavors brought to the Kwanza table often come from the foods found in Africa as well as places Africans were taken, such as America, the Caribbean, and South America. Common ingredients include black-eyed peas, turnip greens, malanga, yams, plantains, name (pronounced naw-may) root, rutabagas, sesame seeds (which star in the Benne Cakes, right), and more.

Among the symbols of Kwanza are the candles, which are lit on seven consecutive nights to represent these seven shared beliefs and values: unity, self-determination, collective work and responsibility, cooperative economics, purpose, creativity, and faith.

There are also three colors of Kwanza:

■ Black symbolizes the African people;
■ Red symbolizes the struggle of the African people;
■ Green symbolizes future and hope.

For a gift idea that integrates the colors of Kwanza with the Mkeka, a straw mat that represents tradition as the foundation on which everything else rests, see page 131.

Benne Cakes
✳

Benne means sesame seeds in Mandingo, a language of West Africa, where these nutty-tasting wafers are thought to have originated. A picture of these chewy cookies, along with a gift presentation idea for Kwanza, appears on page 131.

- 1 cup packed brown sugar
- ⅓ cup butter, softened
- 1 egg
- 1 teaspoon lemon juice
- ½ teaspoon vanilla
- ¾ cup all-purpose flour
- ¼ teaspoon salt
- ⅛ teaspoon baking powder
- 1 cup toasted sesame seeds

Preheat oven to 325°F. Beat brown sugar and butter in a medium mixing bowl with an electric mixer on medium speed until creamy. Add egg, lemon juice, and vanilla; beat until combined. Beat in flour, salt, and baking powder. Using a wooden spoon, stir in sesame seeds.

Drop dough by rounded teaspoons 2 inches apart on parchment-lined cookie sheets.

Bake in the preheated oven for 12 to 14 minutes or until edges are browned. Transfer to wire rack; let cool. Makes 26 cookies.

treasured
holiday
desserts

Angelic Chocolate Torte

This year, we dug deeply into our files to find all-time favorite desserts that have brought joy to holiday tables for decades. The collection includes Better Homes and Gardens® prizewinners and perennial favorites of our food editors. Enjoy!

Angelic Chocolate Torte

✳

Here's a showstopping way to indulge in chocolate around the holidays.

- ½ cup all-purpose flour
- 1 teaspoon baking powder
- ⅛ teaspoon salt
- 1 cup butter (no substitutes), softened
- 1¼ cups granulated sugar
- 6 egg yolks
- 1 teaspoon almond extract
- 1 cup ground toasted almonds
- 4 ounces unsweetened chocolate, grated
- 6 egg whites
- ¼ cup cherry liqueur or amaretto
- 1 recipe Roman Icing and Filling (below right)
- 1 recipe Meringue (far right) Fresh, chocolate-covered, or maraschino cherries; chocolate-dipped almonds; and/or chocolate curls (optional)

Preheat oven to 350°F. Grease and flour two 9x1½-inch round baking pans. Stir together flour, baking powder, and salt; set aside.

Beat butter in a large mixing bowl with an electric mixer on medium speed about 30 seconds. Add granulated sugar and beat until fluffy. Beat in egg yolks and almond extract. Add flour mixture; beat on low speed until well combined. Stir in almonds and chocolate. Wash and dry beaters thoroughly.

Place egg whites in a large clean bowl; beat with an electric mixer on high speed until stiff peaks form (tips stand straight). Fold in about one-fourth of the beaten egg whites to lighten batter; fold in remaining egg whites. Pour into prepared pans.

Bake in the preheated oven for 35 to 40 minutes or until a toothpick inserted into the center comes out clean. Cool 5 minutes on wire racks. Remove from pans; cool completely.

To assemble, place one cake layer on a cake plate; brush with half of the liqueur. Top with half of the Roman Filling. Remove meringue from pan; peel off paper. Place meringue on top of Roman Filling; Spread with the remaining Roman Filling. Place second cake layer on top; brush with remaining liqueur. Frost top and sides of cake with Roman Icing.

Garnish with some reserved piped icing, fresh or chocolate-covered cherries or maraschino cherries, chocolate-dipped almonds, and/or chocolate curls, if desired. Chill in refrigerator at least 4 hours before serving. Makes 16 servings.

ROMAN ICING AND FILLING: Beat together one 8-ounce package cream cheese, softened; one 3-ounce package cream cheese, softened; and 1 cup butter or margarine in a large bowl with an electric mixer on medium to high speed until light and fluffy. Beat in 1 teaspoon almond extract. Gradually beat in 7½ to 8 cups sifted powdered sugar, beating to a thick spreading

consistency. (Reserve ¼ cup to pipe as decorative garnish, if desired.) Remove 1¾ cups more to a smaller bowl, and stir in ¾ cup chopped candied cherries; reserve this mixture for filling. For icing, beat 4 ounces semisweet chocolate, melted and cooled, into remaining cream cheese mixture.

MERINGUE: Preheat oven to 300°F. Lightly grease bottom and sides of an 8x1-inch round cake pan. Line bottom with waxed paper. Lightly grease waxed paper. Set pan aside. Place 2 egg whites and 1 teaspoon vanilla in a medium mixing bowl; beat with an electric mixer on low speed until frothy. Add ¼ teaspoon cream of tartar and beat on medium speed until soft peaks form (tips stand straight). Gradually add ⅔ cup granulated sugar, beating at high speed until stiff peaks form. Spoon into prepared pan, smoothing top with back of a spoon to even surface. Bake in the preheated oven for 45 minutes. Turn off oven; let dry in closed oven for 1 hour.

MAKE-AHEAD TIPS: Store frosted cake, covered, in refrigerator up to 3 days. For longer storage, bake cakes as directed; cool completely but do not fill or frost. Place cakes on baking sheet and freeze until firm; place in 2-gallon freezer bags; freeze up to 3 months. Before serving, thaw at room temperature for several hours; fill and frost as directed. Prepare meringue up to 1 day ahead; wrap tightly in plastic wrap and store at room temperature.

Pumpkin-Pecan Pie

Raisin Cream Pie

Your grandmother might have made this pie—it first appeared in Better Homes and Gardens® magazine in 1953. It's wonderfully rich, delightfully old-fashioned, and if you bake at all, you probably have the ingredients on hand.

    1 recipe Pastry for Single-Crust Pie
       (below left)
    3 slightly beaten eggs
    1 cup sugar
    2 tablespoons lemon juice
    2 tablespoons butter or
       margarine,* melted
   ½ teaspoon ground cinnamon
   ½ teaspoon ground nutmeg
   ¼ teaspoon salt
    1 cup raisins
   ½ cup chopped walnuts

Preheat oven to 375°F. Prepare pastry and line the pie plate as directed.

Stir together eggs, sugar, lemon juice, butter, cinnamon, nutmeg, and salt in a medium mixing bowl. Add raisins and walnuts; mix just until combined. Pour raisin-nut mixture into the pastry-lined pie plate.

Bake in the preheated oven about 30 minutes or until center is set. Cool on a wire rack. Cover and refrigerate within 2 hours. Makes 8 servings.

*Note: Nothing beats the flavor and richness that butter adds to baked goods. However, if you decide to use margarine as an option for butter, use a product that contains at least 80 percent vegetable oil or fat; avoid using any margarinelike products that have less than 80 percent oil or fat, as these contain additional water and milk solids that can change the texture of your desserts.

108

Pumpkin-Pecan Pie

Choosing between pumpkin and pecan pie at the holidays isn't always easy. When this recipe appeared in 1965, the editors loved the way it resolved the holiday pie dilemma—and people have been loving it ever since.

    1 recipe Pastry for Single-Crust Pie
       (right)
    3 slightly beaten eggs
    1 15-ounce can pumpkin
   ¾ cup sugar
   ½ cup dark-colored corn syrup
    1 teaspoon vanilla
   ¾ teaspoon ground cinnamon
    1 cup chopped pecans
       Whipped cream (optional)

Preheat oven to 350°F. Prepare pastry and line the pie plate as directed.

Combine eggs, pumpkin, sugar, corn syrup, vanilla, and cinnamon in a mixing bowl; mix well. Pour into pastry-lined pie plate. Sprinkle with the pecans.

Bake in the preheated oven for 50 to 55 minutes or until a knife inserted off center comes out clean. Cool on wire rack. Refrigerate within 2 hours; cover for longer storage. If desired, serve with whipped cream. Serves 8.

PASTRY FOR SINGLE-CRUST PIE: Stir together 1¼ cups all-purpose flour and ¼ teaspoon salt in a large bowl. Cut in ⅓ cup shortening using a pastry blender until pieces are pea-size. Sprinkle 1 tablespoon cold water over part of the mixture; gently toss with a fork. Push moistened dough to the side of the bowl. Repeat moistening dough, using 1 tablespoon cold water at a time, until all the dough is moistened (4 to 5 tablespoons cold water total). Form dough into a ball. Use your hands to slightly flatten dough on a lightly floured surface. Roll dough from center to edges into a circle about 12 inches in diameter. To transfer pastry, wrap it around the rolling pin. Unroll pastry into a 9-inch pie plate. Ease pastry into pie plate, being careful not to stretch pastry. Trim pastry to ½ inch beyond edge of pie plate. Fold under extra pastry. Crimp edge as desired. Do not prick pastry.

Sweet Mince Cake

✳

Mincemeat is a wonderfully old-fashioned chopped apple and raisin filling. Find it with pie fillings at the supermarket.

- 2 cups all-purpose flour
- 1 teaspoon baking powder
- ½ teaspoon ground nutmeg
- ½ cup apple juice
- ¼ cup brandy or apple juice
- ¼ cup whipping cream
- 1 cup butter, softened
- 1 cup granulated sugar
- 4 eggs
- 1 9-ounce package condensed mincemeat, crumbled (2 cups)
- 2 tablespoons all-purpose flour
  Sifted powdered sugar
  Candied cherries (optional)

Preheat oven to 325°F. Grease and flour one 10-inch fluted tube pan; four 5¾x3x2-inch loaf pans; or three 7½x3½x2-inch loaf pans; set aside. Combine the 2 cups flour, the baking powder, ½ teaspoon salt, and nutmeg; set aside. In another bowl, combine ½ cup apple juice, ¼ cup brandy or apple juice, and cream; set aside.

Beat butter with an electric mixer on medium to high speed for 30 seconds; gradually beat in granulated sugar. Add eggs, one at a time, beating well after each addition. Add flour mixture and juice mixture alternately to egg mixture, beating on low speed after each addition until just combined.

Stir together crumbled mincemeat and the 2 tablespoons flour until mincemeat is separated and coated with flour; fold into batter. Turn into prepared pan(s). Bake in preheated oven 45 to 50 minutes or until toothpick inserted off center comes out clean. Cool in pan(s) on wire rack 10 minutes. Remove from pan(s). Cool completely. Sprinkle with powdered sugar. Garnish with halved cherries, if desired. Serves 16.

Sweet Mince Cake

freezing your family's heirloom holiday desserts

Sometimes those splattered and dog-eared recipe cards passed down through the generations don't tell you how to freeze the treats. Here are some general guidelines.

■ CAKES (unfrosted layer, angel food, sponge, and chiffon): Freeze up to 3 months. To freeze, place cooled cake on baking sheet; freeze until firm. Wrap and seal cake in moisture- and vapor-proof wrap or place in freezer bags. Thaw at room temperature.

■ CHEESECAKES: Freeze whole cheesecakes up to 1 month, individual slices up to 2 weeks. Carefully transfer cooled cheesecake to a freezer-safe plate. Place whole cheesecake in a freezer bag. Place individual pieces in an airtight container. Thaw whole cheesecake in the refrigerator overnight, or pieces at room temperature for 30 minutes.

■ FRUIT PIES (baked): Freeze up to 4 months. To freeze, cool completely; transfer to a self-sealing freezer bag. Thaw at room temperature; reheat, covered, in a 325°F oven.

■ FRUIT PIES (unbaked): Assemble pie in a metal or freezer-to-oven plate. Place in a self-sealing freezer bag. Use tapioca for thickener in the filling (for every 2 tablespoons flour, substitute 1 tablespoon quick-cooking tapioca; for every 4 teaspoons of cornstarch, substitute 1 tablespoon quick-cooking tapioca). Freeze up to 4 months. Bake, covered, in a 450°F oven for 15 minutes; reduce temperature to 375°F and bake for 15 minutes more. Uncover; bake 55 to 60 minutes or until bubbly.

■ CREAM, CUSTARD, AND MERINGUE PIES are not recommended for freezing.

Choclava

Preheat oven to 350°F. Grease a 2-quart rectangular baking dish; set aside. Stir together flour, the ¾ cup brown sugar, and the baking powder in a large mixing bowl. Add milk; mix well. Stir in the chopped pitted dates; spread the batter in the prepared baking dish.

Stir together boiling water, pecans or walnuts, the ¾ cup brown sugar, the butter or margarine, and vanilla in a medium mixing bowl; pour over the date mixture in the baking dish.

Bake, uncovered, in the preheated oven for about 30 minutes or until set. Serve warm with unsweetened whipped cream, if desired. Serves 12 to 16.

Date Pudding

✴

This crowd-pleasing home-style favorite is super-simple—it makes its own sweet sauce as it bakes. Try serving it with a dollop of unsweetened whipped cream for a contrast to the sweetness of the pudding.

1   cup all-purpose flour
¾   cup packed light brown sugar
1   teaspoon baking powder
½   cup milk
1   cup chopped pitted dates
1¼ cups boiling water
1   cup chopped pecans or
    walnuts
¾   cup packed light brown sugar
1   tablespoon butter or margarine
1   teaspoon vanilla
    Unsweetened whipped cream
    (optional)

Choclava

✴

Baklava, a classic Greek pastry, gained widespread popularity in the U.S. in the early 1900s. Of course, it wasn't long before a chocolate lover came up with a way to add some chocolate to the mix— and a new classic was born.

4   cups walnuts, finely chopped
    (1 pound)
1   cup miniature semisweet
    chocolate pieces
¾   cup sugar
1½ teaspoons ground cinnamon
1¼ cups butter, melted
1   16-ounce package frozen phyllo
    dough, thawed
¾   cup orange juice
½   cup sugar
½   cup water
½   cup honey
2   tablespoons lemon juice
2   ounces semisweet chocolate
    (optional)
2   tablespoons water (optional)

Preheat oven to 325°F.

For filling, stir together walnuts, the 1 cup chocolate pieces, the ¾ cup sugar, and the cinnamon in a large bowl; set aside.

Brush the bottom of a 15x10x1-inch baking pan with some of the melted butter. Unfold phyllo. Layer 8 of the phyllo sheets in the pan, brushing each sheet with butter and allowing the phyllo to extend up sides of pan. (To prevent phyllo from drying out, keep sheets covered with a slightly moistened cloth until ready to use.) Sprinkle about 2 cups of the nut mixture over phyllo in pan.

Top with another 4 sheets of the phyllo, brushing each with more of the melted butter. Sprinkle with 2 more cups of the nut mixture and top with 4 more phyllo sheets, brushing each sheet with butter.

Top with remaining nut mixture and remaining phyllo sheets, brushing each sheet with butter. Drizzle any remaining butter over top layer. Trim edges of phyllo to fit pan. Using a sharp knife, cut into diamond or triangle-shape pieces, cutting to but not through the bottom layer.

Bake in the preheated oven for 45 to 50 minutes or until golden brown. Immediately finish cutting diamonds or triangles. Cool slightly in pan on a wire rack.

Meanwhile, combine orange juice, the ½ cup sugar, the ½ cup water, the honey, and lemon juice in a medium saucepan. Bring to boiling; reduce heat. Simmer, uncovered, for 20 minutes. Pour over warm choclava in pan. Cool completely.

To serve, if desired, heat and stir the 2 ounces chocolate and the 2 tablespoons water in a heavy, small saucepan over low heat until smooth. Drizzle some of the chocolate mixture over each piece of choclava. Store in the refrigerator. Makes about 60 pieces.

110

Date Pudding

Walnut Cream Roll

✳

A quintessential Victorian dessert, cake rolls often found their way onto Midwestern farmhouse tables in the last century. Here, a deliciously nutty layer of cake spirals around lots of light and airy whipped cream for a dessert that surely made a hardworking farm family feel very special.

    4   egg yolks
    4   egg whites
    1   teaspoon vanilla
    ½   teaspoon salt
    ½   cup granulated sugar
    ¼   cup all-purpose flour
    ½   cup finely chopped walnuts
        Powdered sugar
    1   cup whipping cream
    2   tablespoons granulated sugar

Preheat oven to 375°F. Grease and flour a 15x10x1-inch baking pan; set aside. Beat egg yolks in a medium bowl with an electric mixer on high speed about 4 minutes or until thick and lemon-colored. Wash beaters thoroughly. Combine egg whites, vanilla, and salt in large bowl. Beat on high speed until soft peaks form (tips curl); gradually add the ½ cup sugar, beating until stiff peaks form (tips stand straight).

Fold yolks into whites; carefully fold in flour and nuts. Spread in prepared pan. Bake in the preheated oven about 12 minutes or until top springs back when lightly touched.

Immediately loosen edges of cake from pan and turn out onto towel sprinkled with powdered sugar. Starting at short side, roll up cake and towel together. Cool on a wire rack.

Meanwhile, beat whipping cream and the 2 tablespoons sugar with an electric mixer on medium speed until soft peaks form. Unroll cake; remove towel. Spread the sweetened whipped cream over cake to within 1 inch of edges. Roll up. Cover and chill up to 2 hours. Makes 10 servings.

Ginger-Pear Galette

Ginger-Pear Galette

✳

It's hard to believe something this beautiful and elegant is so simple. Maybe that's why it became one of our favorites.

    ½   of a 17½-ounce package
            (1 sheet) frozen puff pastry
    1   slightly beaten egg white
    2   tablespoons all-purpose flour
    2   tablespoons granulated sugar
    2   tablespoons brown sugar
    1   tablespoon finely chopped
            crystallized ginger
    1   teaspoon finely shredded
            lemon peel
    2   tablespoons butter
    3   large pears, halved, cored,
            peeled, and thinly sliced
        Whipped cream (optional)
        Crystallized ginger (optional)

Thaw puff pastry according to package directions. Roll out pastry to 14x11-inch rectangle on a lightly floured surface. Trim to a 12x10-inch rectangle. Place on a parchment-lined baking sheet. Prick pastry with a fork. Cut ½-inch-wide strips of pastry from scraps and fit onto edges of rolled rectangle of pastry, like a picture frame. Press slightly to adhere.

Brush edges with egg white. Decorate edges with cutouts from the pastry trimmings, if desired. Brush pastry again with the egg white. Stir together the flour, granulated sugar, brown sugar, the 1 tablespoon crystallized ginger, and the lemon peel. Cut in the butter until pieces are the size of small peas.

Preheat oven to 400°F. Sprinkle half of the ginger mixture over pastry. Arrange pear slices on top, overlapping slightly. Sprinkle with remaining ginger mixture.

Bake, uncovered, in the preheated oven for 15 to 18 minutes or until the pastry is golden brown and the pears are tender. Serve warm. If desired, top with whipped cream and additional crystallized ginger. Makes 8 servings.

Mulled Cranberry Cider

Buffalo Wings with
Blue Cheese Dip

112

Crimson-Glazed
Ham Balls
and Smokies
(see recipe, page 114)

Potato and Leek Soup
(see recipe, page 114)

Put your timesaving crockery cooker on overtime during the holidays! It's perfect for everything from festive party fare and quick after-shopping suppers to a terrific soup with leftover ham.

'tis the season for *slow* & *easy* cooking

Buffalo Wings with Blue Cheese Dip

✱

Check out how easy it is to bring a sports-bar favorite home for the holidays! Serve with crisp celery sticks and lots of napkins.

- 16 chicken wings (about 3 pounds)
- 1½ cups bottled chili sauce
- 3 to 4 tablespoons bottled hot pepper sauce
- 1 recipe Blue Cheese Dip (right) or bottled ranch salad dressing

Cut off and discard wing tips. Cut each wing into 2 sections. Rinse chicken; pat dry. Place chicken on the unheated rack of a broiler pan. Broil 4 to 5 inches from the heat about 10 minutes or until chicken is browned, turning once. Transfer chicken to a 3½- or 4-quart crockery cooker.

Combine chili sauce and hot pepper sauce; pour over chicken wings. **Cover and cook** on low-heat setting for 4 to 5 hours or on high-heat setting for 2 to 2½ hours. Serve chicken wings with Blue Cheese Dip or bottled ranch salad dressing. Makes 32 appetizers.

Nutrition facts per piece with 1 tablespoon Blue Cheese Dip: 108 cal., 8 g total fat (3 g sat. fat), 21 mg chol., 217 mg sodium, 3 g carbo., 0 g fiber, 6 g pro.

BLUE CHEESE DIP: Combine one 8-ounce carton dairy sour cream; ½ cup mayonnaise or salad dressing; ½ cup crumbled blue cheese (2 ounces); 1 clove garlic, minced; and 1 tablespoon white wine vinegar or white vinegar in a blender container. Cover and blend until smooth. Store dip, covered, in the refrigerator for up to 2 weeks. If desired, top dip with additional crumbled blue cheese before serving. Makes 3 cups.

Mulled Cranberry Cider

✱

- 1 small orange
- 8 cups cranberry-raspberry drink
- ¼ cup packed brown sugar
- 6 inches stick cinnamon
- 3 star anise
- 1 teaspoon whole cloves

Remove orange portion of orange peel using a vegetable peeler. Cut peel into strips. Squeeze juice from orange; discard seeds and pulp. Combine orange juice, fruit drink, and sugar in a 3½-, 4-, or 5-quart crockery cooker. **Place peel,** cinnamon, anise, and cloves on a double-thick, 8-inch square of 100-percent-cotton cheesecloth. Bring corners of cloth together; tie with a clean cotton string. Add to cooker. **Cover; cook** on low-heat setting for 5 to 6 hours or on high-heat setting for 2½ to 3 hours. To serve, remove spice bag and discard. Ladle cider into cups. If desired, garnish with additional peel, anise, or cinnamon sticks. Serves 10.

Nutrition facts per 6-ounce serving: 152 cal., 0 g total fat (0 g sat. fat), 0 mg chol., 30 mg sodium, 37 g carbo., 0 g fiber, 0 g pro.

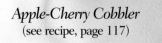

Apple-Cherry Cobbler
(see recipe, page 117)

114

Crimson-Glazed Ham Balls and Smokies

✳

With ground ham and cranberries, this recipe takes an all-time favorite to new gourmet heights. Pictured on page 112.

1 egg, beaten
½ cup finely crushed graham crackers
¼ cup finely chopped onion
2 tablespoons snipped dried cranberries
2 tablespoons milk
  Dash ground cloves
8 ounces ground pork
8 ounces ground cooked ham
  Nonstick cooking spray
1 16-ounce can jellied cranberry sauce
1 12-ounce bottle chili sauce
1 tablespoon vinegar
½ teaspoon dry mustard
1 16-ounce package small fully cooked smoked sausage links

Preheat oven to 350°F. For meatballs, combine the egg, crackers, onion, cranberries, milk, and cloves in a large mixing bowl. Add pork and ham. Shape into 3 to 4 dozen ½-inch meatballs.

Lightly coat a 15x10x1-inch baking pan with nonstick cooking spray. Place meatballs in pan. Bake for 15 minutes or until no longer pink inside. Drain.

Stir together cranberry sauce, chili sauce, vinegar, and dry mustard in a medium saucepan. Cook over medium heat until sauce is melted, stirring occasionally. Combine meatballs and sausage in a 3½- to 5-quart crockery cooker. Pour sauce over meatballs and links. Cover; cook on high-heat setting for 2 to 3 hours. Serve immediately or keep warm on low-heat setting for up to 2 hours. Serve with toothpicks. Makes 25 appetizers.

Nutrition facts per serving: 138 cal., 7 g total fat (2 g sat. fat), 29 mg chol., 524 mg sodium, 13 g carbo., 1 g fiber, 6 g pro.

Potato and Leek Soup

✳

Here it is! Your delicious fix-and-forget solution to what to do with leftover holiday ham. Pictured on page 112.

3 cups water
1 1.8-ounce envelope white sauce mix
1 28-ounce package frozen loose-pack diced hash brown potatoes with onion and peppers
3 medium leeks, sliced (about 1 cup total)
1 cup diced Canadian-style bacon or cooked ham
1 12-ounce can evaporated milk
½ teaspoon dried dillweed or 1 teaspoon snipped fresh dillweed
1 8-ounce carton dairy sour cream
  Snipped fresh parsley or dillweed (optional)

Gradually stir water into white sauce mix in a 3½- or 4-quart crockery cooker until mixture is smooth. Stir in potatoes, the 3 leeks, Canadian-style bacon, evaporated milk, and dillweed.

Cover and cook on low-heat setting for 7 to 9 hours or on high-heat setting for 3½ to 4½ hours.

If using low-heat setting, turn to high-heat setting. Stir about 2 cups of the hot potato mixture into the sour cream. Return sour cream mixture to cooker. Cover and cook about 10 minutes more on high-heat setting or until heated through. Ladle into bowls. If desired, sprinkle with parsley or additional dillweed. Serves 10 to 12.

Nutrition facts per serving: 212 cal., 10 g total fat (5 g sat. fat), 28 mg chol., 476 mg sodium, 23 g carbo., 1 g fiber, 8 g pro.

Apple-Cherry Cobbler

✳

Great news—you can make the Spiced Triangles up to 24 hours in advance. That will free up oven space on the day of your holiday celebration.

½ cup granulated sugar
4 teaspoons quick-cooking tapioca
1 teaspoon apple pie spice
1½ pounds cooking apples, peeled, cored, and cut into ½-inch slices (4½ cups)
1 16-ounce can pitted tart cherries
½ cup dried cherries
1 recipe Spiced Triangles (below) Ice cream, such as butter pecan or cinnamon; or half-and-half; or light cream (optional)

Stir together sugar, tapioca, and apple pie spice in a 3½- or 4-quart crockery cooker. Stir in the apple slices, undrained canned cherries, and dried cherries until combined.
Cover; cook on low-heat setting for 6 to 7 hours or on high-heat setting for 3 to 3½ hours. To serve, divide cherry-apple mixture among 6 to 8 shallow dessert dishes. Top with Spiced Triangles and ice cream, half-and-half, or light cream, if desired. Serves 6 to 8.
Spiced Triangles: Preheat oven to 375°F. Combine 1 tablespoon sugar and ½ teaspoon apple pie spice in a bowl. Unroll 1 package (8) refrigerated crescent rolls. Separate triangles. Brush tops with 1 tablespoon melted butter and sprinkle with sugar-spice mixture. Cut each triangle into 3 triangles. Place on an ungreased baking sheet. Bake in the preheated oven for 8 to 10 minutes or until bottoms are lightly browned. Remove to a wire rack to cool. Cover and store, tightly covered, up to 24 hours at room temperature.

Nutrition facts per serving: 387 cal., 11 g total fat (3 g sat. fat), 5 mg chol., 333 mg sodium, 75 g carbo., 3 g fiber, 4 g pro.

Dilled Pot Roast

✳

After a day of shopping, come home to this hearty supper that's ready and waiting in your crockery cooker.

1 2- to 2½-pound boneless beef chuck pot roast
2 tablespoons cooking oil
½ cup water
1 teaspoon dried dillweed
1 teaspoon coarse salt (kosher) or ¾ teaspoon regular salt
½ teaspoon pepper
½ cup plain yogurt
2 tablespoons all-purpose flour
3 cups hot cooked noodles

If needed, cut roast to fit into a 3½- to 4-quart crockery cooker. Brown roast on all sides in hot oil in a large skillet. Transfer to cooker. Add the water to cooker. Sprinkle roast with ¾ teaspoon of the dried dillweed, the salt, and pepper.
Cover and cook on high-heat setting for 5 to 6 hours or on low-heat setting for 10 to 12 hours until meat is tender. Transfer roast to a serving platter, reserving juices; cover roast and keep warm. Pour cooking juices into a glass measuring cup; skim off fat. Measure 1 cup of the reserved juices.
For sauce, stir together yogurt and flour in a small saucepan until well combined. Stir in the 1 cup reserved cooking juices and remaining dillweed. Cook and stir until thickened and bubbly. Cook and stir 1 minute more. Serve meat with sauce and noodles. Makes 6 to 8 servings.

Nutrition facts per serving: 373 cal., 12 g total fat (4 g sat. fat), 136 mg chol., 443 mg sodium, 22 g carbo., 2 g fiber, 41 g pro.

seasonal crockery cooker tips

■ For holiday cooking, call on crockery cooker recipes to free up rangetop and oven space.

■ When entertaining, keep hot beverages simmering in your cooker on the low-heat setting during your party.

■ To tote foods to potlucks in your cooker: After the food is completely cooked, wrap cooker in heavy foil or several layers of newspaper. Place cooker in an insulated container. The food should stay hot for up to 2 hours (do not hold longer than 2 hours). Once at the party, plug in the cooker; the food will stay warm on the low-heat setting for a few more hours.

■ To get a jump-start on preparations the night before: Cut up or chop all of the vegetables and the meat. Combine the seasonings and liquids. (Note: Do not precook meats unless they are to be fully cooked before adding to the cooker.) Place vegetables, meat, and seasonings in separate containers; cover and refrigerate. The next day, place ingredients in order specified in the recipe into the cooker. Cover; cook as directed.

115

Dilled Pot Roast

Get the whole family involved in decking the halls (or at least the windows, walls, and roof!) of this holiday house. Besides creating a beautiful decoration for your home, you'll create memories and a meaningful tradition for years to come.

gingerbread house *party*

This year, why not gather your favorite people together to create something beautiful? Our holiday Gingerbread House relies on a clever array of colorful candies for its decorations (rather than elaborate piping bags and star tips). This means that once you bake and assemble the house, youngsters can help with the fun stuff—placing the candies following the ideas in the picture, *opposite,* or following the whims of their own imaginations.

tips of the building trade

- If you wish to use your enlarged patterns again in the future, consider laminating them.
- When rolling dough, lightly flour the rolling pin rather than covering it with a pastry cloth. This makes for a smoother surface on the cookie pieces.
- Keep any frosting not in use covered, in the refrigerator, so it won't harden.
- Always let frosting dry thoroughly between construction steps.
- If the roof starts to slip before it dries, put a glass underneath the eaves to hold the roof in place until it dries.
- Avoid heavy candy on the roof. The house may collapse under the weight.
- When the holiday season is over, set your gingerbread house out in the yard for squirrels and birds to nibble on.

Gingerbread Cookie Dough

✳

1½ cups shortening
1½ cups sugar
1 tablespoon baking powder
1 tablespoon ground ginger
1½ teaspoons baking soda
1½ teaspoons ground cinnamon
1½ teaspoons ground cloves
1½ cups molasses
3 eggs
3 tablespoons vinegar
7½ cups all-purpose flour
2 recipes Royal Icing (below right)
   Variety of candies, wafer
      cookies, and candy canes

Beat shortening in a very large mixing bowl with an electric mixer on medium to high speed for 30 seconds. Add sugar, baking powder, ginger, baking soda, cinnamon, and cloves; beat until combined. Beat in molasses, eggs, and vinegar. Beat in as much flour as you can with the mixer. Stir in any remaining flour with a wooden spoon. Divide dough into four equal portions. Cover with plastic wrap and chill for 3 hours or until dough is easy to handle.

Meanwhile, enlarge pattern pieces on page 121 as directed. Cut out house ends, sides, and roof. If desired, cover pattern pieces on both sides with clear adhesive plastic to protect them. Lightly grease the back of a 15x10x1-inch baking pan. If desired, place pan on a damp towel to prevent it from sliding around.

Preheat oven to 375°F.

Roll one portion of the dough with a lightly floured rolling pin to a thickness of slightly less than ¼ inch on the greased pan. (Roll dough in the general shape of the piece to be cut.) Place a front pattern piece on dough. Cut around piece with a sharp knife.

Remove excess dough. (Save scraps for rerolling; cover and refrigerate scraps.) Remove pattern; leave dough cutout on the pan. Bake in the preheated oven for 10 to 12 minutes or until edges are lightly browned and center is just firm.

Leaving gingerbread on the pan, cool slightly (about 3 minutes). Place pattern piece on the warm, baked cookie piece and trim edges exactly. Return gingerbread to oven and bake 3 minutes more or until very firm. Cool 3 minutes on pan. Loosen bottom of cookie piece with a flat, metal spatula. Cool completely on pan; transfer to wire racks.

Repeat rolling and baking steps for the second front piece and for the 2 sides. For the roof, knead refrigerated scraps together to blend colors. Divide in half. Roll and bake as directed for the other pieces to make two roof pieces.

Decorating and assembly: If you allow gingerbread pieces to dry overnight, they will be even firmer and better for construction. Prepare 1 batch Royal Icing. To pipe icing, place some in a sealable plastic bag. Snip off a small corner of the bag. While gingerbread pieces are lying flat, pipe a line of icing for holiday lights. Immediately sprinkle icing line with small candies. Let stand for about 2 hours or until icing is dry.

Working on a wooden tray or cutting board (house will be hard to move after this point), pipe icing along the edges of an end and a side. Press the pieces together, holding them in place with short glasses, measuring cups, or heavy coffee mugs. Add remaining side, then end, piping icing on edges to be attached. Keep the supports in place until the icing has dried and pieces are secure (at least 2 hours).

For the roof, pipe or spread icing along the top edges of the house. Set one roof piece into place, using straight pins to hold roof until icing has dried.

Repeat with remaining roof piece. Let dry thoroughly. Remove pins.

Prepare another batch of icing. Use candies and cookies to decorate the sides and front of house to make doors, windows, and other garnishes; attach them with icing. Let stand for about 2 hours or until icing is dry.

Continue frosting the roof until roof is covered with icing; add gumdrops while icing is still wet. Next, attach candy canes to corners of house using dabs of icing. For a final touch, spread additional icing on roof peak. While icing is still wet, attach peppermint candies on edges in a row. Let stand for about 2 hours or until icing is dry.

Store house in a cool, dry location.

Royal Icing

✳

You will need 2 batches of this icing to decorate the house.*

3 tablespoons meringue powder
⅓ cup warm water
1 16-oz. package powdered
   sugar, sifted (4½ cups)
1 teaspoon vanilla
½ teaspoon cream of tartar

Combine meringue powder, water, powdered sugar, vanilla, and cream of tartar in a small mixer bowl. Beat with an electric mixer on low speed until combined, then on high speed for 7 to 10 minutes or until very stiff. Use at once. When not using icing, keep it covered with clear plastic wrap and refrigerate to prevent it from drying out. Makes 3 cups.

*Note: Because the icing hardens quickly, it's best to make the two batches separately—one batch before constructing the house, and the other before decorating it. Keep any icing not in use covered in the refrigerator.

here's how...

1

Roll dough on the bottom of a 15x10x1-inch baking pan. Place the pattern on the dough; cut out with a sharp knife. Then, bake the cutouts directly on the pan (that way, you don't have to move the large, unbaked cutouts).

2

Pipe a generous line of royal icing along the edges to be joined. Short, heavy glasses help hold pieces in place while the frosting dries.

3

Pipe Royal Icing around the top edges of the sides and ends of the house and add the roof pieces. Decorate the roof after positioning it on the house.

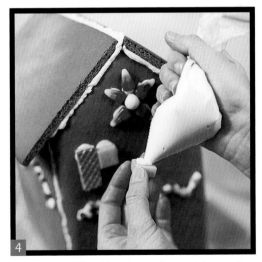

4

For some candies, it's easier to pipe the icing on the piece of candy before attaching it to the house. For other candies, it's easier to pipe the icing on the house first, then attach the pieces. Tip: If you don't like the placement of a piece of candy, let it dry a little, then scrape it off with a straightedge and try again.

deft decorations

■ No need to stick to the candies we used! Consider these decorating options—and keep an eye out for other sweet bits and bobs that might also work:

licorice
Tootsie Rolls
ribbon candy
candy corn
red hots
jelly beans
gumdrops
mini marshmallows
M&Ms
rock candy
almond slivers
peanuts
Neco wafers
candy canes
peppermints
pretzels
ice cream cones
sugar cubes
gum
graham crackers and
    other crackers
breadsticks
Hot Tamales
Tart & Tinys
sugar wafers
small frosted wheat biscuits
gingersnaps
Life Savers
chocolate thin mints

The smaller, more detailed decorations, such as the Tart & Tinys, top, are best done while the pieces are lying flat, before house is assembled. The roof, above, should be decorated after assembly.

Larger decorations, such as the sug wafers, far left, and the candy corns left, can be added once the house assembled and the icing joining its parts is dry. You may need to hold these candies into position a few seconds to set them in place.

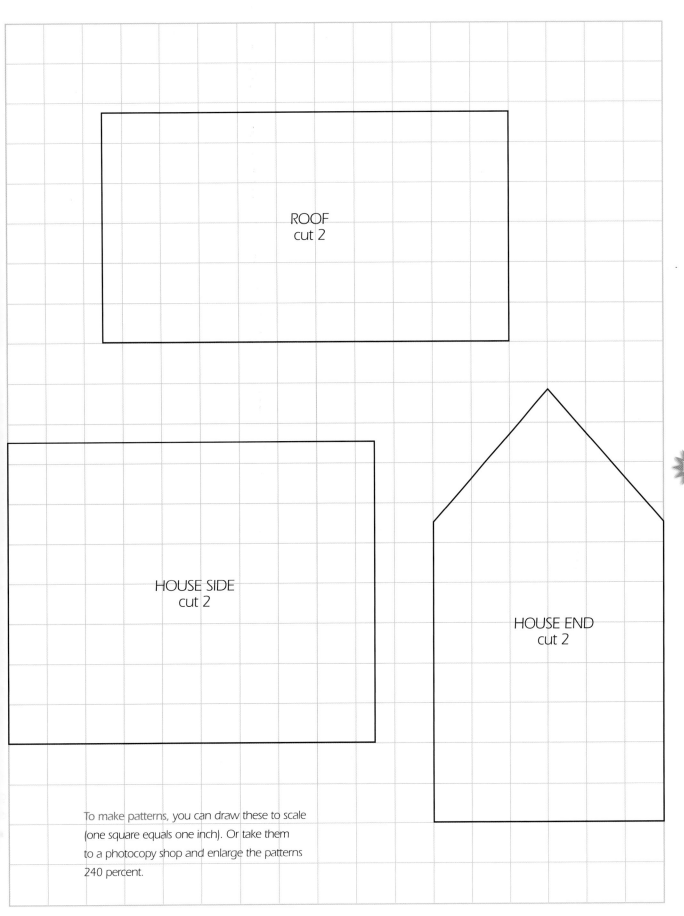

ROOF
cut 2

HOUSE SIDE
cut 2

HOUSE END
cut 2

To make patterns, you can draw these to scale
(one square equals one inch). Or take them
to a photocopy shop and enlarge the patterns
240 percent.

1 SQUARE = 1 INCH

from the HEART

Handmade gifts are treasured for the love and thoughtfulness they convey. Delight your family and friends with gifts that acknowledge their interests and talents—cooking, sewing, collecting, teaching, friendship, and more. An attractively wrapped tray of assorted treats may make the day for a busy teacher or coworker, a stoneware bowl filled with rosemary will delight a gourmet cook, embellished picture frames can display memorable photos or cards, and a box made from recycled greeting cards is a lasting decoration. Experience the joy of sharing this season.

Microwave Candy-Bar Fudge

At the end of a beautiful day of celebration and planning with family and friends, ensure that each person goes to bed with visions of sugar plums and sweet dreams. Everyone decorates the living spaces, yet many forget the place where we spend a third of our day—safely tucked all snug in our beds. The wonderful wreaths and the enchanting linens that adorn these bedrooms offer a festive atmosphere and a good night to all. Enjoy the holiday nights.

...and to all a
GOOD

NIGHT

sweet *dreams*

A few quick additions, whether understated and elegant or bright and bold, allow you or your guests to wake up with the reminder of what a magical season this truly is.

red-y for bed

🌿 It's the simplest way to prepare a guest room for holiday visitors—toss a few extra pillows on the bed. Red pillows, shams, and pillowcases in various shapes, patterns, shades, and sizes warm this room better than a wood-burning stove. Centered over the bed, a wreath of tallowberries and greens eliminates any doubt that this room was prepared especially for the holidays.

To make a wreath quickly, like the one shown here, start with a purchased tallowberry wreath. (Use the wreath later with the greenery, or substitute eucalyptus or other non-seasonal materials.) Place fresh variegated greens behind the wreath, securing them to the wreath form with U-shape floral pins or wire. Keep the shape of the wreath casual and slightly irregular to contrast with the perfectly packed tallowberries.

lean and green

🌿 Crisp white-as-snow linens are inviting any time of year. For the holidays, add touches of green that are equally fresh and clean. On the headboard, a small swag offers the scent of evergreens. To cut boughs of mixed greenery to make a swag like this one, select those with slightly arched branches. Crisscross the stems of the boughs and wire them together. Cover the wire and stems with a bow of sheer white wire-edge ribbon. To attach the swag to the headboard without scratching the finish on the bed, use a chenille strip that matches the bed. For a final surprise, wrap a bedtime treat in a small gift box and nestle it among the pillows.

cornucopia wreath

The sunburst design
s dramatic wreath
pan the seasons.
nble it easily using
cones, a wire form,
ragrant eucalyptus.

here's how...

1

Prepare the paper. Cut the paper into fifteen 6×10-inch pieces. Place the small end of the plastic foam cone about 1¼ inches from a corner. Roll the paper around the cone, keeping the paper edge straight alongside the cone.

2

Shape the cones. Hold the paper around the cone with pins. Run a bead of glue under the top edge of the paper, about ¼ inch from the edge. Press the edges of the paper to seal. Allow the glue to cool; remove the pins and cone. Make 15 cones.

153

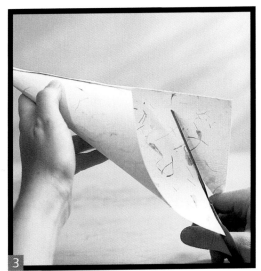

3

Trim the points. Trim away the extending corner for a graceful cornucopia shape.

For a gluing surface, place kraft paper on a work table. Cover the kraft paper with waxed paper and center the wire wreath form on the papers.

4

Attach the cones. Place a large puddle of glue from the center to across the outer ring and, one at a time, press a cone into the glue. Peel away waxed paper.

Glue small embellishments, such as buttons, charms, and ribbons, to the cones. Glue a large embellishment to the center of the wreath. Glue eucalyptus sprigs into each cone.

SHOPPING LIST

⅔ yard red thermal fleece
⅓ yard blue-green
   thermal fleece
7×9-inch piece of blue
   thermal fleece
7×9-inch piece of yellow
   thermal fleece
white No. 5 perle cotton
large-eye
   embroidery needle
18-inch pillow form

❧ Decorate a child's bedroom, a guest bedroom, or a family room with colorful reminders of winter fun. These warm and cozy, easy-to-make pillows will have everyone who sees them dreaming of crisp winter days spent building the tallest snowman or tossing the most snowballs.

Assemble the pillow covers using thermal fleece, which requires no seam finishing and means that you will finish in less time. Cut out the shapes and attach them with running and blanket stitches.

154

hands-on pillow

here's how...

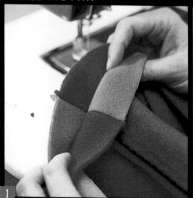

1 Make the pillow front. Cut two 10-inch squares each from the red and the blue-green fleece. Sew the squares together in a four-square pattern, using ½-inch seam allowances. Cut a 19-inch square from red fleece for the pillow back.

2 Place the mittens. Using the pattern on *page 157*, cut a blue and a yellow mitten; reverse to cut two more mittens. Center the mittens on the squares, thumbs pointing inward. Use a blanket stitch to sew the mittens to the squares.

3 Assemble the pillow. With right sides facing, sew the pillow front to the pillow back with a ½-inch seam allowance, leaving an opening in one side. Turn the cover to the right side, insert the pillow form, and slip-stitch the opening closed.

fleecy fellow

SHOPPING LIST

2—13×17-inch pieces of
  blue thermal fleece
8×10-inch piece of white
  thermal fleece
blue-green thermal fleece:
  1×18-inch strip for scarf,
  scraps for mittens
scraps of black and orange
  thermal fleece
two ½-inch-diameter black
  buttons (eyes)
2—3-inch long twigs
No. 3 perle cotton: black,
  white, and red
1¾ yards white ball trim
12×16-inch pillow form

Build the snowman. Use the patterns on *page 156* to cut three snowballs from white, a hat from black, mittens from blue-green, and a nose from orange fleece. Arrange and pin the snowballs to the blue background; pin the scarf behind the snowman's neck area. Sew a running stitch using black perle cotton around the snowman, catching the scarf in the stitches.

155

Add the small pieces. Sew the hat on the snowman and pillow front using white perle cotton. Stitch the nose in place with white perle cotton. Position the mittens, using the twig lengths as a guide, and stitch them to the background with red perle cotton. Sew on the button eyes. Loop the scarf and fringe the ends.

Attach the snowball trim. Pin ball trim to the pillow front, aligning outer edges. Make a tuck in the flange of the trim to round the corners. Baste the trim to the pillow front. Sew the pillow front to the back, leaving an opening in one side. Turn the cover right side out, insert the pillow form, and slip-stitch the opening closed.

Give him some arms. For each mitten, slip one end of a twig under the center snowball. Fit the opposite end of the twig under the mitten.

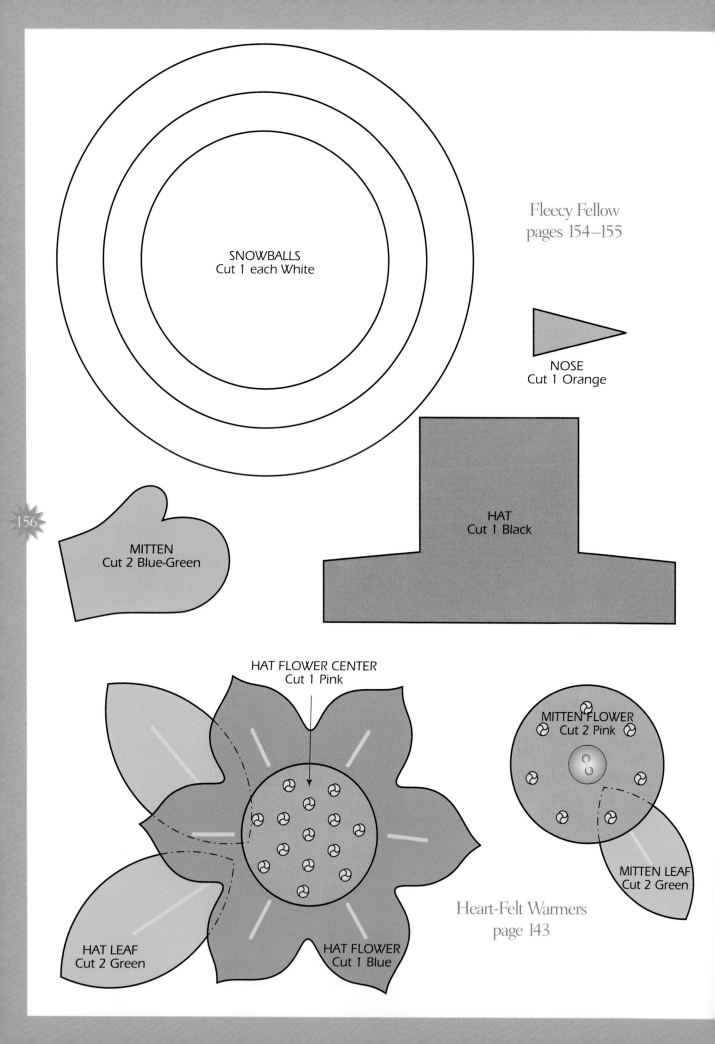

SNOWBALLS
Cut 1 each White

Fleecy Fellow
pages 154–155

NOSE
Cut 1 Orange

HAT
Cut 1 Black

MITTEN
Cut 2 Blue-Green

156

HAT FLOWER CENTER
Cut 1 Pink

MITTEN FLOWER
Cut 2 Pink

MITTEN LEAF
Cut 2 Green

Heart-Felt Warmers
page 143

HAT LEAF
Cut 2 Green

HAT FLOWER
Cut 1 Blue

Patterns are 100% size
unless otherwise noted.

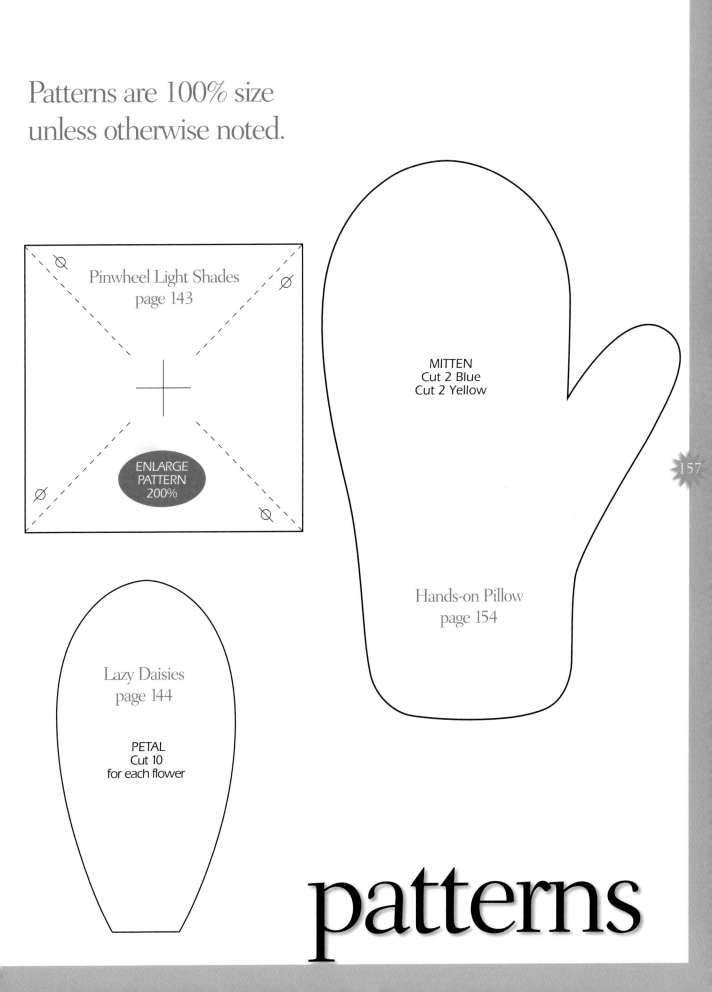

Pinwheel Light Shades
page 143

ENLARGE
PATTERN
200%

MITTEN
Cut 2 Blue
Cut 2 Yellow

157

Hands-on Pillow
page 154

Lazy Daisies
page 144

PETAL
Cut 10
for each flower

patterns

credits & sources

Styling by Marisa Dirks and Jilann Severson and photos by Peter Krumhardt except as follows:

cover, page 4: photo, Peter Krumhardt
page 7: design, Rebecca Jerdee; photo, Jon Jensen
page 8: design, Brian Bolke; photo, Colleen Duffley
page 9: top: photo, William Stites; bottom, design, Breaca Lozier and Libby Becker
pages 10–11: designs, Breaca Lozier and Libby Becker
pages 12–13: designs, Cody Evitt; photos, Hopkins Associates
page 14: top: design, Breaca Lozier and Libby Becker; bottom: design, Lorna Call; photo, Perry Struse
page 15: illustrations, Tom Rosborough
page 16: top: design, Marisa Dirks and Jilann Severson; bottom: photo, Hopkins Associates
page 17: top right: photo, Hopkins Associates; top left: design, Jilann Severson; bottom right and bottom left: photo, Hopkins Associates
pages 18–21: designs, Sherry J. Bloom; photos, Hopkins Associates. Leaf lace skeletons available through Tom Thumb Workshops, 59 Market St., Onancock, VA 23417, 800/527-6502; www.tomthumbworkshops.com
pages 22–23: designs, Breaca Lozier and Libby Becker
pages 24–25: designs, Gina Harrell; photos, Lark Smotherman
pages 26–27: designs, Jim Williams; photos, Tom McWilliam
page 28–29: designs, Cherri Colby; photos, Jim Hedrich, Hedrich-Blessing
page 30: top left: design, Beth D. Stevens; bottom left: design, Wendy Elaine Johnson; photo, Andy Lyons
page 31: top right: design, Sue Banker; photo, Hopkins Associates; center: photo, Hopkins Associates; lower right: design, Rebecca Jerdee; photo, Alise O'Brien
page 33: photo, Jon Jensen
pages 34–35: photo, Hopkins Associates
pages 36–37: photos, Jon Jensen
pages 38–39: designs, Cody Evitt; photos, Hopkins Associates

pages 40–41: designs, Wade Scherrer
page 42: design, Margaret Sindelar; photo, Perry Struse
page 43: photo, Perry Struse
page 44: design, Inga Johns; photo, Perry Struse
page 45: photo, Perry Struse
page 46: design, Rebecca Jerdee; photo, Michael Garland
page 47: design, Julyette Marshall; photo, Marcia Cameron
pages 48–51: designs, Rebecca Jerdee; photos, Jon Jensen; how-to photos, Peter Krumhardt
page 52–57: top: designs, Shari Kinkaid; photos, King Au
page 58: top left: design, Jim Williams; right: design, Paula Marshall; lower left: design, Sharri Kinkaid, photo, King Au
page 59: left center: design, Mary de Buhr; photo, Perry Struse; bottom left: photo, Perry Struse
pages 60–61: designs, Jacqueline Winch
page 62: top: design, Marj Hubner; photo, Perry Struse. Stampendous rubber stamps and stamping supplies available from Outstamping Designs, 215 5th St., West Des Moines, IA 50265; 515/277-5719. Bottom: designs, Niki Eschen; all photos, Peter Krumhardt
pages 63: design, Sue Banker; photo, Hopkins Associates
pages 65: food stylist, Charles Worthington
pages 69: food stylist, Lynn Blanchard; photo, Andy Lyons
pages 70: food stylist, Pouke; photo, Colleen Duffley
pages 71: food stylist, Charles Worthington; photo, Scott Little
pages 72: food stylist, Pouke; photo, Colleen Duffley
pages 73: food stylist, Brooke Leonard; photo, Mark Thomas
pages 74: food stylist, Charles Worthington
pages 77: food stylist, Lynne Gagne; photo, Tony Glaser
pages 78—79 (center): food stylist, Charles Worthington
pages 80–85: food stylist, Charles Worthington
pages 86–87: photos, Craig Anderson
pages 88–89: designs, Breaca Lozier and Libby Becker
pages 90–92: designs, Lorna Call; photos, Hopkins Associates
pages 93: photo: Hopkins Associates
page 94: top left: design, Wade Anthony; photo, Michael Garland; center: design, Lynda Sutton; photo, Eric Roth; bottom left: designs, Cherri Colby; photos, Jim Hedrich, Hedrich-Blessing

page 95: top center: photo, Judith Watts; left: design, Lynda Sutton, photo, Eric Roth; top right: design, Jim Williams; photo, Tom McWilliam; bottom center: design, Gina Harrell, photo, Lark Smotherman; bottom left: design, Wade Anthony; photo, Michael Garland
pages 98: food stylist, Pouke; photo, Colleen Duffley
pages 99: food stylist, Charles Worthington
pages 103: food stylist, Charles Worthington
pages 112: food stylist, Charles Worthington
pages 119: food stylist, Charles Worthington
page 122: photo, Perry Struse
page 130: top center: food stylist, Charles Worthington; top left: food stylist, Charles Worthington; lower left: food stylist, Pouke; prop stylist, Karen Johnson; photo, Colleen Duffley
pages 131: food stylist, Charles Worthington
page 132–133: photos, Perry Struse
page 134: photo, Mike Dieter
page 135: photos: Perry Struse
page 136: design, Jim Williams; photo, Perry Struse
page 137: top: photo, Perry Struse; bottom: design, Jim Williams; photo, Perry Struse
page 138: photos, Perry Struse
page 139: top: design, Rebecca Jerdee; photo, King Au; bottom: photo, Perry Struse
pages 140–142: designs, Kim Jankowiak and Peggy Pepper; photos, Jon Jensen
page 143: left and center: photo, Jon Jensen; right: designs, Sue Banker; photo, Hopkins Associates
page 144: designs, Kim Jankowiak and Peggy Pepper; photos, Jon Jensen
page 145: designs, Cindy Kuhn; photos, Alise O'Brien
pages 146–147: designs, Rebecca Jerdee; photos (146), Peter Krumhardt; photo (147), Michael Garland
pages 149: design, styling, Rebecca Jerdee; photo, Alise O'Brien
page 150: design, Cindy Kuhn; photo, Alise O'Brien
page 151: design, styling, Rebecca Jerdee; photo, Alise O'Brien
pages 152–153: design, Rebecca Jerdee; photo, Alise O'Brien; how-to photos, Peter Krumhardt
page 154–155: photos, Peter Krumhardt

index

index *continued*